MARC NÖLK

NEURO
ATHLETICS

——— **FOR RIDERS**

INNOVATIVE EXERCISES THAT TRAIN YOUR
BRAIN AND CHANGE YOUR NERVOUS SYSTEM
FOR OPTIMAL HEALTH AND PEAK PERFORMANCE

TRANSLATED BY HELEN MCKINNON

TRAFALGAR SQUARE
NORTH POMFRET, VERMONT

First published in the English language in 2023 by
Trafalgar Square Books
North Pomfret, Vermont 05053

Originally published in the German language as *Neuro Athletik für Reiter* by Franckh-Kosmos Verlags-GmbH & Co. KG, Stuttgart

Disclaimer of Liability
The author and publisher shall have neither liability nor responsibility to any person or entity with respect to any loss or damage caused or alleged to be caused directly or indirectly by the information contained in this book. While the book is as accurate as the author can make it, there may be errors, omissions, and inaccuracies.

Trafalgar Square Books encourages the use of approved safety helmets in all equestrian sports and activities.

ISBN: 978 1 64601 178 0
Library of Congress Control Number: 2022948561

Photographs by Anna Auerbach/KOSMOS
Diagrams and drawings by KOSMOS Kartografie, Stuttgart (p. 16), Atelier Krohmer (p. 47), and Cornelia Koller/KOSMOS (pp. 11, 13, 18, 33, 36, 42, 43, 61)

Design by Peter Schmidt Group GmbH, Hamburg
Cover design by RM Didier
Index by Michelle Guiliano, DPM (linebylineindexing.com)
Typefaces: Frutiger, Garamond Premiere

Printed in China

10 9 8 7 6 5 4 3 2 1

☞ *Table of Contents*

1   "I Play with Brains"

....

4   **WHAT IS NEURO-RIDER TRAINING?**
5   "Riding Isn't a Sport"
5   Concussions Can Be Deceptive
8   What Does Neuro-Rider Training Do?
8   Not "One Size Fits All" Training
12 Our Brains Are Always Doing Three Things
16 Perception of Safety
18 Releasing the "Brakes"
18 Common Brake Boosters
22 When the Nervous System Takes It Too Far

24 Allies for Survival
26 Systems that Control Movement

....

39 **PREPARING FOR NEURO-RIDER TRAINING**
39 Caution! Contraindications
40 Success Is Difficult without a Goal
41 Perfect Execution
42 Target the Right Area
42 Slow Motion or High Speed?
43 The Dose Makes the Medicine
43 Stop When It Feels Good
43 Always Feel the Movement
45 Fuel and Activation

46 THE FOUNDATION—TESTING AND RETESTING

47 The Principle: Test–Drill–Retest
47 Test Yourself
48 Changes with Brain Speed
48 Tests for Training at Home
49 Testing the Drills
51 Forward Bend
52 Scarecrow
53 Half Snow Angel
54 Shoulder Flexion
54 Pistol Rotation
56 Zombie Stand
57 Intensified Zombie Stand
58 One-Legged Zombie Stand
59 Walk the Line
59 Hand RAPS
61 Pain

61 Test Other Movements
63 The Test Is Part of the Training

....

64 NEURO-RIDER MOVEMENTS— LET'S GO!

65 Physical Awareness or Proprioception
65 Training Your Physical Awareness
68 Tongue Drills
70 Neutral Standing Position with the Spine Long
72 Isometric Muscle Contraction
72 Head Drills
83 Thoracic Spine Drills
86 Lumbar Spine Drills
91 Hand Drills
92 Shoulder Drills
94 Hip Drills
97 Leg Drills
100 Isometric Full Body Contraction

126 EXERCISES FOR THE VESTIBULAR SYSTEM— WELL-BALANCED!

127 Balance and Equilibrium

130 Hourglass

132 Giant Wheel with Gaze Stabilization

132 Vestibulo-Ocular Reflex in Eight Directions

135 Nodding "Yes" and "No" with Gaze Stabilization

136 Heel Bounces with Gaze Stabilization

136 Figure Eights with Gaze Stabilization

....

138 EXERCISES FOR THE RESPIRATORY SYSTEM— BREATHE BETTER

139 Neuro Exercises for Your Respiratory System

139 Breathing through a Straw

140 360-Degree Breathing

141 Breathing with a Band

142 Breathing Ladder

143 Seated Diaphragm Stretch

144 Air Hunger

145 Breathing into a Bag

....

146 NEURO-RIDER TRAINING— QUESTIONS AND ANSWERS

147 Shaping Your Neuro-Rider Training

147 How Long, How Often, How Much?

147 The Laissez-Faire Approach

149 The All-In Approach

149 Be Your Own Biggest Fan— Sustainable Learning and Training

151 Increase the Level of Difficulty

151 Questions Are Good!

153 Final Words

....

155 INDEX

102 NEURO-RIDER VISION—SEE BETTER

103 Training Your Visual System

103 Better Vision for Posture and Stability

107 Gaze Stabilization at Nine Points

108 Gentle Gaze Tracking in Eight Directions

110 Saccades

112 Optokinetics

114 Cross-o-Matic or Pencil Press-Up

115 One-Eyed Cross-o-Matic

117 Eye Circles

118 Peripheral Vision

120 Near-Far Jumps

121 Inhibition Instead of Activation

122 Pinhole Glasses

123 Colored Glasses

123 Binasal/Uninasal Partial Occlusion

124 Earplugs

"I PLAY WITH BRAINS"

Marc Nölke

"So, what do you do?"—that too-common question people are always asking at parties. I hate it and usually start muttering something incomprehensible.

"Dad, what are you doing at the barn?"
"Do you help scared ski jumpers to jump again?"
"What's the name for your job?"

My son, on the other hand, deserved a straight answer. I tried: "I play with brains. I find out where brains are tired and where they are working too hard."

"So, where is mine tired?"
"Yours isn't worn out—it's great!"
"And what about if you find the tired bit, what then?"

"Then I help people find an exercise that will get the tired part fit and healthy again. I teach them so much that at some point they know enough not to need me anymore."

"You are what you think.
All that you are arises from
your thoughts."

Gautama Buddha, Dhammapada

From the ski jump to the barn.

WHY I WROTE THIS BOOK

Competitive sports are bad for you. They nearly killed me. When I was 18, an equipment defect resulted in a serious fall at the Winter Olympics in Albertville, France. While my teammates were in the Théâtre des Cérémonies celebrating the opening ceremony, I was in the operating room, having emergency surgery for internal injuries. I had lost my dream of a lifetime, and nearly my spleen, too. The sudden loss of purpose and goals, not to mention the injuries, hit me like a sledgehammer. The 20-centimeter-long scar on my abdomen healed, but the severe concussion became a problem later.

Concentration problems, letters dancing in front of my eyes, headaches. All the doctors cleared me, but I still felt totally out of it. Everyday life was chaotic, and even driving became dangerous. For example, I once missed a warning sign and crashed into a hole on a building site. Anxiety and depression followed and stayed with me for the next 20 years. I knew nothing about the mechanisms behind my injuries and their delayed effects. If only I had known then what I know now ... if only, if only ... but there's no point looking back. It took me a long time to find my way back to myself. Curiosity and stubbornness helped me. I was able to travel the world and learn from the best teachers. I have since achieved my lost Olympic victory as a trainer.

All in good time.

Every rider should know the brain has the potential to heal even into advanced age, and movements will improve on the way there. That is why I wrote this book.

Marc Nölke

In this book, I will usually refer to riders as women. My intention is to make the text clear and easy to read, while addressing issues that affect all of us, regardless of gender or identity. This linguistic shortcut is for simplicity's sake and isn't intended to carry any deeper meaning.

WHAT IS NEURO-RIDER TRAINING?

"RIDING ISN'T A SPORT"

I come from a family of riders. The women hung out at the barn, with me in the weight room. Sometimes I was allowed on a horse, but I always just cantered around, which the women didn't seem to appreciate.

"Riding isn't a sport," I'd say. "The horse does all the work. Do some fitness training!"

"Marc, you haven't got a clue!" they'd reply. "And anyway—when, exactly? We don't have time!"

The women didn't want to hear it. After all, who's interested in the opinions of a 13-year-old? For me, it was crystal clear—they could be better if they trained their own bodies as well as their horses. And riding would also be safer for them. However, this thought only came to me much later.

As a ski jumper, I knew that if you are messing around, unprepared, not warmed up, unfit, or your mind is elsewhere, you'll soon end up falling. And it's no different with riding, except you'll fall off a horse and not a ski jump.

Accidents can be caused by external circumstances, by your own errors, or by a combination of both. However, ski jumpers have perfect control over their bodies. Horses all over the world are ridden by people who lack even basic skills. They can move their bodies with precision around the supermarket, but not in extreme situations. The risk of accidents increases because these people are less able to respond to unexpected problems.

I can picture my mother in the hospital, her upper arm completely shattered, full of wires and suspended in traction on a hospital bed. Her face was swollen and bruised, blue and green. Could the fall have been avoided if she trained her mind and body *off* the horse to be more fit on him? It's a shame to have to give up something you love. You lose a part of yourself. I know that.

CONCUSSIONS CAN BE DECEPTIVE

Bam! The two pounds in your head are flung back and forth like Jello in a bowl. Your brain function may be disturbed for a short time afterward.

"What's your name? What day is it today? What year is it? Do you feel sick?"

Even if somebody has symptoms, diagnostic imaging such as computerized tomography (CT) scans or magnetic resonance imaging (MRI) usually do not reveal any visible findings. The deceptive thing is that, as the result of a chain reaction of metabolic responses and inflammations, the brain enters an "energy crisis" that can last for several weeks.

The consequence is slow changes in the brain. It's equally deceptive that it happens so slowly that the patient doesn't associate the symptoms with the concussion. Strange things happen—and you don't know why (Pearce et al. 2015; Giza and Hovda 2014; Simpson-Jones and Hunt 2019).

Constant tiredness. Pulse rate through the roof. Anxiety. Needing to wear glasses. Headaches. Dizziness. Even worse, a diagnosis of Parkinson's disease may follow two or three years later. It's not unusual, and the link is proven (Gardner et al. 2018; Abu

Talh et al. 2017; Delic et al. 2020). Like rugby players, downhill skiers, motorcycle racers, and racecar drivers, horseback riders are in a group of athletes at high risk for concussions. But do you know how fit the other athletes in this group are? And how hard they train themselves physically and mentally? That's why they usually recover well. This is not the case with riders. Riders suffer for a long time. And most riders don't know anything about the possible long-term consequences.

PREVENTION

There are millions of riders in the world, both active and occasional. Consider how many potential concussions that can be per year! How many people ride through life with long-term consequences?

Prevention isn't sexy, that's for sure. But what if you could get even better and have even more fun riding by training in ways that would reduce accidents? What if your horse would thank you for it if he could?

☞ CONCUSSIONS IN RIDERS

A US study surveyed 115 riders, all of whom had experienced a fall as well as several head injury symptoms. 44% revealed that they had been concussed at least once. They reported the following symptoms (Kuhl et al. 2014):

Neck pain 63.8%	Headaches 56.4%
Dizziness 43.6%	Poor balance 27.7%
Difficulty concentrating 24.5 %	Loss of consciousness 23.4%
Tiredness 23.4%	Irritability 23.4%
Feeling of slowing down 20.2%	Numbness/tingling 19.1%
Brain fog 17.0%	Memory problems 17.0%
Sensitivity to light 16.0%	Nausea 16.0%
Blurred vision 14.9%	Sensitivity to sound 13.8%
Sleepiness 12.8%	Vomiting 10.6%
Ringing ears 10.6%	Amnesia 10.6%
Sadness/depression 8.5%	Problems sleeping 8.5%

...brating disposable toothbrush held against the upper arm improves the rider's perception of the arm, enabling ...o control it better.

Gait analysis is an essential test that gives the trainer lots of information.

WHAT DOES NEURO-RIDER TRAINING DO?

You can use what I call "Neuro-Rider Training" to work on specific issues or to improve your overall performance. You can focus on:

— Coordination and fine-tuning of the aids
— Body symmetry
— Head posture
— Hand position
— Anxiety in certain situations
— Inappropriate/unhelpful emotions
— Inappropriate emotional responses
— Difficulties with rhythm
— Uneven hips
— Shoulder crookedness
— Focus and concentration

NOT "ONE SIZE FITS ALL" TRAINING

I know you want a plan for solving your problems. Everybody wants a plan. Ready-made plans sell well, and for some people, those plans work. But for many people, they don't. For many people, even the best training plans based on the latest scientific findings and experts' experience do nothing. *Nada. Niente.* How can that be?

You might think this is down to not following a plan correctly, or a lack of willpower or consistency. And in one sense, that's true, but it isn't quite that simple. Human brains and bodies may be similar overall, but when it comes down to the details, they're as individual as our fingerprints.

This is because we all have lived different lives, had different or no experience with personal training, eat differently, have different hormone levels, and have suffered different injuries, had different accidents, and overcome different illnesses. Each of these factors potentially affects the nervous system. When you realize this, it should become clear that the same training plan or the same exercise obviously cannot work equally well for everybody.

You won't get any plans here. Sorry. You also won't get a "magic pill" that will do the job for you. Positive outcomes happen remarkably often, but it's impossible to say whether, when, or how fast, because there are far too many different factors in play.

My friend Zachariah Salazar has taught martial arts, guitar, philosophy, physiology, and personal training for 40 years. He says: "People accept that it takes ten years to learn to play the guitar well. They accept that it takes ten years to earn a black belt in karate. They realize that you can't grasp philosophy in a year. But when it comes to health and fitness, they want pills and six-week programs. Health and fitness need to be earned, just like you need to earn a black belt in karate."

Please look at this book as a starting point. It isn't a black belt or a six-week program. You will learn to make better decisions for your health, riding, and general fitness.

In the pages ahead, I'm going to present a selection of exercises, called "drills." You can find out which exercises are right for you by testing them out. I describe how

Even if riders' errors are similar ...

... their ways of solving problems usually aren't.

9

Flexibility test: The forward bend.

Balance test: Standing on one leg—this test was over after three seconds.

that works in chapter 2, The Principle—Testing and Retesting (p. 47).

Testing and retesting are an important part of the training process. Please be willing to experiment and look at it as a game.

Every physical activity you've done in your life so far—jogging, stretching, yoga, tai-chi, tango, zumba, CrossFit, soccer, or even "active sitting," such as on a balance ball, affects your nervous system in some way. However, I think it's very important to understand exactly *how* these tools affect your nervous system, and why they might be helpful or unhelpful.

OBJECTIVES

My aim is for you to have learned the following by the end of this book:

— What stimuli there are, and how they differ.
— How the most important body movement control systems work together and influence each other.
— How to recognize your own critical problems and weaknesses.
— Which stimuli are the right ones for you, and how to decide for yourself how and where you start your individual training and what to include in it.
— How to solve your own problems.

"CIB" EFFECTS

I have already seen many riders cry. Magic moments happen when communication between rider and horse is smooth and relaxed—it's fun! But along with the direct effects on riding, Neuro-Rider Training can also have other, more indirect effects. I call them "CIB effects," because clients and

Neuro-Rider Training	Classical Training
Teaches principles	Teaches discipline
Following rules or free play	Usually prescribed processes with more linear structure, and rigid pattern
Testing and experimenting	Planned specification of content before the training process
Fun	Consistency
Automatically gives constant feedback	No feedback, only checks on training
Constant feedback and constant adaptation	Feedback and adaptation only during occasional checks on performance
Variable behavior is encouraged	Planned behavior is required

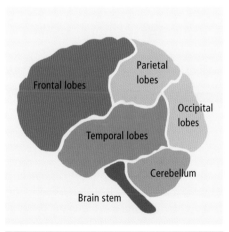

Areas of the brain as seen from the outside. However, the stark visual divisions between areas aren't accurate to reality: all areas of the brain work together.

graduates of my seminars always ask "Could It Be?" questions—for example:

— "Last night I slept through the night again—could it be because of my mental training?"
— "I can see better when I'm driving at night—could it be because...?"
— "I can concentrate much better at work—could it be because...?"
— "I haven't had any migraines for six weeks—could it be ...?"

— "I'm losing weight even though I'm still eating as much—could it be because...?"

— "My psoriasis is much better—could it be because...?"

— "I'm much more relaxed with my horse—could it be...?"

— "My horse hasn't had any issues with 'X,' 'Y,' 'Z' since I started—could it be ..."

— "I feel like I can think much more clearly—could it be ..."

— "I hardly have any emotional outbursts anymore—could it be...?"

... and many more.

And the answer to every "CIB" question is yes! Give your brain the input it longs for, and it will be happy. When your brain is happy, everything works much better. So expect a few CIB effects, and keep looking inside yourself, because if you develop and strengthen the basic neuronal prerequisites for movement, everything in your life will be easier.

OUR BRAINS ARE ALWAYS DOING THREE THINGS

This is obviously a highly simplified description of the brain, but it's essentially correct in its broad strokes, and useful for understanding training and for putting the exercises in this book into practice in the right way.

1. THE BRAIN RECEIVES INPUT FROM THE BODY AND THE ENVIRONMENT

This input comes from *receptors*, that is, small sensors situated in the layers of our skin, and in our muscles, tendons, ligaments, and even bones. These receptors supply our brain with information about the movement of our limbs and their position in relation to each other. We also have receptors to monitor chemical changes in the body and temperature changes.

For example, oxygenation from inhaling changes the pH value of our blood, and these changes in pH value in turn control the respiratory system. The retinas of our eyes have light-sensitive photoreceptors that provide input for the visual system. The sensors for sound waves and the hopefully highly sensitive sensors for acceleration and gravity—the metronomes for the vestibular system—are in our inner ears.

2. THE BRAIN PROCESSES AND INTERPRETS INPUT AND MAKES DECISIONS

Like the boss of a large company who's always checking and evaluating the completeness of reports from various sites and departments, the brain makes decisions about what to do next based on the data it receives, and its own data processing. All of this happens "under the radar" of your conscious perception.

3. THE BRAIN PRODUCES OUTPUT

"Output" here can come in lots of forms: An intentional or unintentional movement with a certain quality; symmetry or asymmetry—a sloping shoulder or a wobbly head when riding; a fast or slow, powerful or inhibited movement; or an emotional outburst.

However, an output can also be something that hurts. Pain is output from the brain. Our digestion and our blood pressure are also outputs from our brain, as are the excretion of hormones and the functions of the immune system.

HOW YOU RIDE ...

These three things—receiving input, processing and interpreting input, and producing output—happen in the brain all the time. They form a self-perpetuating cycle. New movements generate new input, which is in turn received and interpreted. On this basis, the brain decides what to do and produces a new output, which in turn generates new inputs, and so on. How you ride is output from your brain.

Think for a minute about your riding. We usually practice movements we want to improve again and again, with conscious effort and conscious control.

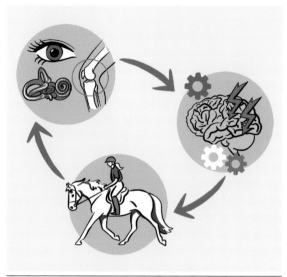

Our brain is always doing three things.

The horse's brain is also always doing these three things. One of the inputs is the rider.

13

ASK YOURSELF

What different, additional, or better input can I give my brain in order to make it happy and help it produce better output? It's a logical question, if you think about it. But despite its simplicity, it hasn't occurred to most people to try changing or adapting the input their brains receive. Later, I will show you a variety of input from the four most important systems of the body and explain how you can identify useful inputs that will improve your output using the test/retest method.

We try to improve the output by training the output. But does that make sense? If we aren't seeing any lasting improvement, shouldn't we change the strategy of "more of the same," and instead consider whether it might make sense to change the input?

LIFE-THREATENING?

The brain's most important job is to keep us alive. There's nothing more important to the brain than ensuring our survival! Isn't that nice? But this also means survival matters more to the brain than jumping your horse over a log or riding elegantly in the dressage arena. These neuronal games aren't systemically relevant.

We have all kinds of survival reflexes, but no reflex to help us ride a piaffe. A piaffe is of absolutely no importance to the brain. It might be important to your ego—the frontal lobes, the area of conscious thought—but as far as the rest of the brain is concerned, it's just messing around.

Reflexes are reserved for actions that can keep us alive.

As far as the brain is concerned, jumping a log isn't going to ensure our survival.

Now we're getting to the point: *The brain lets us perform any movement, without any problems and with maximum strength, if it thinks that movement is safe. And for the brain, whether an activity is assessed as "safe" depends on the quality of the input, its interpretation of the input, and the predictions it models based on that input and that interpretation.* The brain is constantly making predictions about the immediate future. To guarantee safety and survival, it isn't enough just to work purely "descriptively"—that is, to work by describing the current situation. Makes sense, doesn't it? If your brain only warned you about danger when you were already in the middle of receiving an impact

> **WE NEED GOOD SIGNALS FROM THE:**
> — Proprioceptive system
> — Visual system
> — Vestibular system
> — Respiratory system

to your head after falling off your horse, it would be too late to do anything about it. Now we come to the next important point: *The better the signals your brain gets from all its receptors, the easier it will find processing and prediction.*

The brain will only allow us to throw ourselves over a jump if it predicts that we'll be safe.

SAFE OR UNSAFE?

The brain takes this giant dataset and compares it with information saved from previous experiences. Then it decides whether you are SAFE or UNSAFE. If your brain assesses the coming situation to be SAFE, it will relax your muscles, reduce your respiratory rate, keep your heart rate steady, and allow your joints to move through their full range of motion.

However, if it assesses the coming situation to be UNSAFE, it will increase muscular tension, respiratory rate, and pulse rate, and you might also experience pain or shortness of breath. Many people experience back pain. What's more, your mental state is instantly influenced by your brain, so you feel anxious. And if your brain keeps detecting UNSAFE situations, you might even become depressed, which serves to avoid threats and keep you safe.

PERCEPTION OF SAFETY

All this means we need to find stimuli that increase our perception of our safety. I'd like to use an example to explain what that means in practical terms: Imagine you tear a ligament in your ankle and rest your ankle for a long time. Your brain hardly receives any signals from the motion sensors in your ankle while you're resting it. The neurons that transfer information from your ankle to your brain are "asleep" and may be asleep for weeks. When neurons stop firing, their connections to each other become weaker. Prior to your injury, the "map" of your ankle in your brain was precise (top left image) but now, after weeks without any activity, it isn't precise anymore (lower left image).

That means your brain no longer knows exactly what position your foot is in; as a result, it can't accurately predict how the foot can bear weight. Is this a good starting point for your brain to ensure your "survival"? Nope! Your brain thinks: "I have no idea what the foot's doing, so I can't guarantee anything." In this context, riding your horse at canter over a log is immediately categorized as UNSAFE, and full power to your body and riding position will not be made available. But that obviously applies to all movements, not just jumping a log.

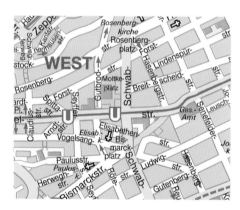

Which map would you rather travel with?

Full speed cross-country with a smile.

And if you nevertheless decide to jump the log, despite your brain's hesitation, your stubborn frontal lobe will go on an ego trip. It *can* work, but only because people are incredibly good at compensating. You can expect your brain to reach for its ultimate emergency brake: pain. But you shouldn't resent it, because it's just trying to protect you. Your brain produces pain because it believes there are too many threatening signals and too few safe signals (G. Lorimer Moseley 2017).

INPUT AND OUTPUT PRINCIPLES

— The brain's most important job is to keep us safe. Safety always comes before performance!

— The brain is always forecasting what will happen next. Adequate and precise input is necessary for accurate forecasts.

— Better input leads to better forecasts, and better forecasting ability leads to better output.

+ **Blood sugar fluctuations**
+ **Oxygen supply**
+ **Eye movements and visual processing**
+ **Old injuries**
+ **Vestibular dysfunction**
+ **Social problems—stress**
+ **Sleep problems**

Identifying and removing "brake boosters."

RELEASING THE "BRAKES"

If we want to improve our performance or our movements, or reduce pain, we need to increase the brain's perception of safety and reduce its perception of danger. First, we need to find and release the threats or "brakes." How do we find these blocking obstacles? Which input do we need to change? There's no standard solution or training plan for this; it's a question that must be answered on a case-by-case basis. But I'll be happy to help you figure out how to narrow it down. First, let's look for obvious potential for "brakes."

COMMON BRAKE BOOSTERS

FUEL SUPPLY PROBLEMS—BLOOD SUGAR

Blood sugar levels like a rollercoaster aren't something brains find cool. Blood sugar levels that are too high or too low make movements uneven, unsteady, and even dangerous (Serra et al. 2009; Khan, Barlow, and Weinstock 2011). When the tank is empty, the brain quickly starts to panic.

FUEL SUPPLY PROBLEMS—OXYGEN

Along with glucose, oxygen is the most important fuel for our brain. Injuries like bruised or broken ribs, illnesses such as asthma or COPD, or even bad habits caused by stress can severely impair the supply of oxygen to the brain. If this happens, neuroplastic change—long-term learning—becomes very difficult. This affects a good two-thirds of my clients, including Olympic athletes.

DEFICIENCY PROBLEMS—EYE MOVEMENTS AND VISUAL PROCESSING

It's important for the brain that our two eyes give it a clear picture of the environment we are in. Slow or inaccurate eye movements slow down perception of our environment. Interpreting visual data requires more calories—takes more effort—when there are too many differences between the images from the right and left eye. If our eyes and visual processing aren't in good shape, the brain steps on the brake.

You'd do that, too, if your windshield wipers stopped working in the rain, wouldn't you? Have you experienced one or more concussions? Are you sensitive to bright light or noise? Does reading make you tired quickly? Do you have to wear glasses or contact lenses? Are you unable to stand packed concert halls, supermarkets, or anywhere busy with crowds of people? Then the cause of your problems could be here.

OLD INJURIES AND "BLURRY MAPS"

Firstly, breaks, torn ligaments, and the like leave behind damaged receptors at the site of injury. Secondly, the reduced flow of information during the period of injury can alter the "maps" in our brain and make them "blurry." Even when the injury has long since healed, it can take a long time for the neuronal representation of the once-injured tissue to be restored in the brain.

If joints don't move through their entire range of movement over a longer period, the mechanoreceptors typically found in the joints suffer an activation deficit that also has a negative effect on the quality of the associated "maps." Would you take your chances in an unknown and dangerous area with a blurry or inaccurate map?

When the mechanoreceptors of the knee aren't sending any good input, output quickly becomes less precise.

1

2

3

1 *Breathing against resistance to symmetrically activate the diaphragm.*

2 *Activating the balance system: Gaze stabilization with rapid head movement.*

3 *Walking in a straight line with the eyes closed: This is a more difficult exercise when done on a wooden beam.*

VESTIBULAR DYSFUNCTIONS

We'll talk about the balance system in our inner ears in more detail later. But for now, what matters is that the brain clearly doesn't like not knowing exactly where gravitational force is coming from and how quickly we're moving. Anybody who's ever been unseated by a bucking horse will know what I'm talking about.

SOCIAL PROBLEMS

People are herd animals. Problems at work and with friends, family, partners, or children are a source of emotional and psychological stress. Stress causes changes to hormone excretions, blood sugar levels, and breathing patterns—which brings us back to our first two brake boosters.

LACK OF SLEEP

Too little sleep is bad—very bad. Not getting enough sleep makes everything worse: mood, libido, vision, balance, sense of movement, reactions, attention, and much more. Important repair and waste disposal measures take place in the brain as we sleep. Sleep is king. So go on, off to bed. Close your eyes. Sleep!

CONCLUSION

When your brain puts on the brakes when you're riding, you should find and eliminate the factors boosting the brakes. You can find the right stimuli to counter your personal set of brakes with the test/retest principle on page 47.

Rolling a tennis ball along the thoracic spine.

Bending and stretching with eye movement.

WHEN THE NERVOUS SYSTEM TAKES IT TOO FAR

Anxiety about riding is something riders don't like to talk about. Everything becomes less fun, becomes a test of courage, and we start avoiding things that trigger our anxiety. We communicate our anxiety to the horse, too. Anxiety makes us overreact and sometimes do strange things—and often those things cause the horse to suffer. But our anxiety is usually based on false assumptions and expectations about future events. We can be anxious about people, animals, things, situations, movements, and pain. Denying or not acknowledging anxiety unfortunately doesn't make the problem any smaller. Quite the opposite.

It's much more helpful to recognize and understand anxiety. The leading scientist in

Leg-yield works much better once the thoracic spine has been mobilized.

the field of anxiety research, Joseph LeDoux, once said: "Anxiety is the price we pay for our brain's ability to imagine the future." I think that sums it up quite well.

Lorimer Moseley from Australia is one of the world's leading scientists looking into the question of what pain is, how pain arises, and, of course, how we can reduce pain. He concisely sums up the results of his research: "Pain is a construct of the brain" (L. Moseley 2011).

Top researchers from both fields agree that pain and anxiety are "output"—that is, they are our brain's *opinions* about the state of the current and future dangerous situation in and around our body.

In the case of fear of heights and vertigo, there are experimental indications that this unpleasant feeling could result from an "intersensory maladjustment if visual information does not correspond to vestibular and proprioceptive information" (Brandt et al. 1980).

It goes without saying that our experiences play a major role in this subconscious formation of opinions, as does the social and cultural milieu that we live in. Context influences perception of anxiety and pain (G. L. Moseley and Arntz 2007). For example, one and the same movement can occur and cause distress in the context of "barn/horses," but cause no distress in the context of "family" or "office"—or vice versa.

Pain (and equally anxiety) warns us about impending danger and the threat of pain, and immediately mobilizes our stress and emergency systems to arm us against that potential threat. However, anxiety and pain aren't necessarily proportional to the degree of actual injury, actual physical harm, or actual threat or danger we're experiencing: We can feel incredible anxiety, capable of paralyzing us, even without being attacked by a real tiger. Knowing there's no realistic chance of falling doesn't stop us from feeling fear of heights. And in the same way, we can feel intense pain even when nothing is wrong. On the one hand, pain and anxiety are important, self-protective feelings—on the other hand, they can be disruptive and unhelpful when they occur frequently and inappropriately. Excitingly, numerous pieces of research show that understanding how these feelings arise can greatly reduce pain and anxiety. Knowledge can therefore be a very effective painkiller and anxiolytic (G. L. Moseley 2004)—and now you know a little more.

ALLIES FOR SURVIVAL

It's helpful to imagine anxiety and pain as friends and allies, because, after all, they only want us to survive. However, sometimes these feelings objectively aren't appropriate to the situation.

A mouse in the tack room is just as unlikely to kill us as a papercut, but both can trigger strong emotions. Pain can become problematic when an injury has long since healed, or when there is objectively no threat. Our "protective system" is working overtime, and protects us unnecessarily, like a "helicopter parent" at the playground, always hovering over their child, ready to needlessly intervene in a game and deny their child opportunities to learn. Many different areas of the brain are involved in these reactions. In pain research, we talk about the "pain neuromatrix" (Melzack, n.d.; G. Lorimer Moseley 2017; Chapman 1996; Legrain et al. 2011).

NEUROMATRIX

Let's take an example: Imagine your grandma for a minute, and think of everything you associate with her. Here, "grandma" is a trigger for other thoughts, feelings, and maybe even physical sensations, just like an old song from our childhood can trigger a cascade of memories and associated feelings. In both cases, very different areas of the brain are activated to a lesser or greater extent. This would be a "grandma neuromatrix," but *your* grandma matrix is guaranteed to be different from *my* grandma matrix. That's also the case for the pain neuromatrix. Pain and anxiety are individual, and always real for the person experiencing them. Saying things like, "Don't make a fuss," or, "It's not that bad," don't help anyone.

Happiness instead of anxiety makes riding fun!

In my experience, it's highly likely that much of your pain and anxiety will be alleviated if you develop your training with this book and practice daily—it's one of the CIB effects that I have already mentioned (p. 11) because your brain gets better input from various systems in your body. Your "maps" become precise—and your brain can navigate more confidently and make better predictions about the future with better maps.

SYSTEMS THAT CONTROL MOVEMENT

Connect four! Dividing the systems we need to talk about into a set of four has advantages because it enables us to better understand each individual system. However, we need to keep in mind that this division doesn't exist in reality. All the areas mentioned are intrinsically linked. They mutually influence each other and are mutually dependent on each other.

When you start training, you should learn the exercises for the four areas separately, and then you should join up the exercises for all four areas as a second step. You'll find more information about this in the last chapter of the book (p. 146).

SYSTEM 1: PROPRIOCEPTION— FEELING

(From the Latin *proprius*, "own," and *recipere*, "to receive.")

The sense of *proprioception* enables us to feel where parts of our bodies are—in relation to each other and in space—without us having to touch or see them. It helps us plan and perform movements without constantly needing to use our vision to find out what our body parts are doing. You can engage your proprioception if you close your eyes, stretch your arms out to the sides, and then use your left index finger to touch first your nose and then your left thumb. You might not quite manage the first time, but it doesn't take much practice. Proprioception is closely linked to our sense of touch.

1

Proprioceptors—receptors for proprioception—are found in muscles and joints all over the body. They respond to stretching and compression (pressure) as well as to changes in the angle of a joint. If proprioception is working correctly, proprioceptors are constantly sending information to the brain so it always knows where individual body parts are at any given time, whether they are moving, and, if they are, how fast and in what direction. For proprioception to work smoothly, muscle tone—the basic tension of the muscles—must be within specific limits. Restricted proprioceptive sensory perception can have many causes, from a leg that has "fallen asleep" through limited movement to arthritis and brain damage. If the brain doesn't perceive parts of the body well enough, we usually also find these areas difficult to move. We call this *sensory motor amnesia* (according to Thomas Hanna, the

creator of "Hanna Somatics"). Sensory motor amnesia occurs whenever our brain stops getting precise information about the actual status of our body. The mechanisms that aid our sensory and motor competence can be disrupted for a variety of reasons and can be partially or completely absent.

The representations of our body in the brain that we've already discussed are the key to understanding proprioception (see p. 26). Proprioception works well and our brain is happy when it has good "maps" of our body.

1 *The hourglass: Head to the right, hips to the left.*

2 *Head back, hips forward.*

3 *Head to the left, hips to the right.*

4 *Head forward, hips back.*

2

3

4

TRAINING ALL THE SYSTEMS

Problems with proprioception are worse if they come accompanied by difficulties with balance, vision, and sense of touch. That's why we train in these areas too!

GOOD MAPS—GOOD MOVEMENTS

What's the best way to improve these movement maps? That's the million-dollar question!

It's best to exercise the areas with the most mechanoreceptors. That means joints!

When we move all our joints at the same time, it's much more difficult for the brain to focus on any one specific area where the

1

2

GET MOVING

Targeted joint mobilizations are the best way to "refresh" our movement maps.

movement map needs to be refreshed. Your own attention, your focus, is therefore extremely important.

To achieve the right focus, we break movements down into focused mobilization and control of individual joints. We learn the ABCs of movement—that is, precise joint movements. We learn motor controls for individual body parts. You will gradually improve all your body maps of every joint. You will learn to move each individual joint precisely according to your needs. Those are the basics.

1 & 2   A wide, full-body rotation requires an efficient interplay of flexors and extensors. Asymmetrical rotational ability reveals a shortcoming in this interplay.

Determining visual acuity.

Can you see as well with your left eye as with your right?

SYSTEM 2: VISUAL SYSTEM—SIGHT

The definition by famous optometrist William Padula on page 32 summarizes all the components of "vision" and its function. There is more to vision than being able to see near and far away objects clearly. Vision has a powerful influence on how we move in our environment, and on our posture, cognition, and feelings. Vision influences our ability to think. But "vision" is not the same as "seeing." When we say "seeing," we usually mean the function of our eyes, but our eyes are "just" pretty cool biological cameras. The actual seeing—"vision"—happens in the brain. Our eyes are part of our brain, but there is a lot more behind them.

The visual system—meaning not just the eyes, but also all the muscles, nerves, and areas of the brain that are used for seeing—can be very successfully trained, with positive effects on the way we move, how we feel, and how we think. Just as we can train and improve our heart, muscles, or abilities such as strength and flexibility, it makes sense to train our vision. If you find yourself thinking: "But I already wear glasses, so I don't need it," then please read on, because there's more to good vision than 100% visual performance as tested by an optician.

MOVEMENT IN TIME AND SPACE

We need to have a good picture of our surroundings if we want to move precisely and avoid accidents. Without an accurate picture, without knowing about obstacles that might be in our way, and without being able to accurately assess the speed of approaching objects or our own speed, we will really struggle to plan our movements and perform them appropriately in space and time. There are three important areas for processing visual information in the brain: the *occipital cortex*, the *superior colliculus* in the midbrain, and the *thalamus*. You could say that there are two built-in programs for vision. The first is for the detailed vision we need when we work at a computer, or for reading and writing.

Figure eight: Alex walks in a figure eight around two cones.

The exercise: Keep going straight while focusing on the visual target and seeing it clearly.

Never look at the ground—you need to see the cones in your peripheral vision

While we're busy using that program to see and understand details, a second visual program is working away in the background—the ambient program. It's called *peripheral vision*, and it covers everything we see around us while we're focusing on something else.

This background program starts running as soon as we're born. Babies can't see what their mother looks like, but they can see movement. The detailed program, by contrast, has to develop more gradually. The brain needs the peripheral vision program to see and anticipate movement, and to be able to move appropriately in space. Unfortunately, we rarely train or even check it, although it is extremely important, especially for riding.

"Vision is a dynamic, interactive process of motor and sensory function, conveyed by the eyes for the purpose of simultaneous organization of posture, movement, and spatial organization, manipulation of the environment, and, to the highest degree, perception and thought."

Dr. William Padula

If riders can see their surroundings more quickly and more accurately, and the areas of the brain that are part of the visual system work more quickly and more accurately, that gives riders more time to act and react. Studies have shown that vision training has a positive effect on cognitive abilities and concentration. The frequency of injuries also decreases, while overall performance improves.

This isn't surprising when you consider the areas of the brain involved in eyesight and the vast amount of information that we take in and have to process via the visual system—no other sensory system sends as much data to the brain. If this data is fundamentally defective, or cannot be processed or integrated successfully, it requires energy, and sports—and life in general—become more strenuous, and potentially even painful. I've known numerous clients whose energy levels have increased considerably as a result of visual training. They were able to concentrate for longer, read for longer, and train for longer, and still had energy at the end of a normal day's work and/or training, instead of being worn out and tired. Where previously they'd sat on their horses crooked and gone through life crooked, they became straight and stable with visual training. Even if you have perfect visual acuity, this doesn't mean that your visual system is working well. You can still easily fail to spot a car in traffic or keys lying on the table in front of you.

SYSTEM 3: VESTIBULAR SYSTEM—BALANCE

In her book *Sensory Integration and the Child*, Anna Jean Ayres encapsulates the importance and integral significance of our sense of balance:

"As long as the body works together as a whole with all its senses, adaptation and learning are effortless for the brain. The sense of balance is the frame of reference that brings everything together. It forms the basic relationships that a person has to gravity and their physical environment.

All other types of sensations are processed with reference to this basic vestibular information."

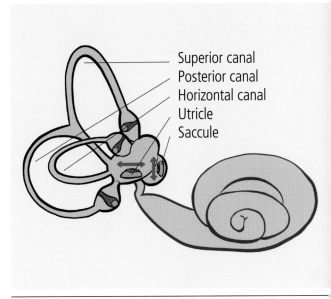

Superior canal
Posterior canal
Horizontal canal
Utricle
Saccule

Which way is down? Where are we going?

The "frame of reference that brings everything together" involves different areas and parts of the brain that work together closely to stop us from constantly falling flat on our faces—an apparently simple task that's much more complex than we give it credit for.

And "frame of reference that brings everything together" means that all areas of the brain want to know where up and down are, how fast we are moving, and where. Our vestibular system delivers this incredibly important information. Although we can't directly feel the sensory perception of our vestibular organs in the same way we can smell an odor or see a color, vestibular signals contribute to a surprising number of brain functions, from automatic reflexes to spatial perception, cognitive functions, and motor coordination (Hitier, Besnard and Smith 2014; Angelaki and Cullen 2008).

Many people have problems with this extremely important system.

A group of researchers in the United

States discovered that 35% of adults over 40 showed signs of vestibular dysfunction. The number of people with balance disorders increases dramatically with age, to up to 85% in eighty-year-olds (Agrawal, Ward and Minor 2013). You could easily conclude that vestibular activation is an important key to healthy mental and physical performance into advanced age. By the way, the standard kinds of fitness training done on machines in gyms offer hardly any exercises for the vestibular system.

Basic data for our sense of balance is provided by a tiny, complex system of receptors that hopefully always does its job meticulously from its well-designed position in the inner ear. I don't want to go into any further detail about the precise anatomy and function of these sophisticated structures, but you should know the basics so you can understand why it can be so crucial to do specific drills in a very specific way.

HOW THE VESTIBULAR SYSTEM WORKS

In each inner ear, we have three *canals* and two *macula organs*—a total of five receptors per side. The canals are shaped like rings, and the macula organs are two small lumps underneath. They're called the *utricle* and *saccule* (the cochlea is responsible for hearing, so we'll leave it out for this purpose). The three canals register the movements of the head:

— The horizontal canals register rotations of the head to the right and left (as when shaking your head "no").
— The anterior canals register forward tilting of the head (to look down at your own chest, for example).
— The anterior canals are activated when we raise our head and tilt it back (to look at a point above you on the ceiling).
— Our wonderful sensors for forward movement and gravity clear up questions such as: "Which way is up and down?" "How fast am I moving, and in which direction?"

The *saccule* is permanently in action in riders. It detects vertical acceleration—movements up and down.

The *utricle* senses acceleration on a horizontal plane—forward, back, to the side, and so on. The saccule, utricle, and canals on each side send their measurement data to the brainstem via a nerve. This data is destined for the headquarters of the vestibular system, the *vestibular nuclei*.

These nuclei are important processing centers, because they also receive information from other systems such as the visual system and proprioceptive system (you'll notice we're back at "input—interpretation—output"). All these inputs are processed, compared with one another, and checked for plausibility here—and corresponding output is generated. The information might not match, which we call a sensory mismatch. This happens in cases of sea sickness, for example. The vestibular nuclei also have other subdivisions that produce output that activates our anti-gravity muscles, for example, or trigger our cardiovascular functions, along with blood pressure changes, or tell our eyes how fast they should look and where.

IN BRIEF

Our movements would be chaos without an accurate vestibular system. Its function is essential. Obviously, the body is able to compensate for a lack of input for a long time. But compensation is not integration—and always comes at a price. The price we pay is muscular tension, deformed bones and joints, and degenerative processes.

A second part of the vestibular system still remains partly unexplored. German cybernetician Hans Mittelstädt called it *somatic graviception* (Mittelstädt 1995)—that is, perception of gravitation by the body. Mittelstädt's experiments gave clear indications that, along with the vestibular receptors, there must be other sensors in the body that are involved in controlling the position of the eyes, neck, and limbs. These receptors are presumed to be in our kidneys and blood vessels. We can activate this somatic balance system with rapid movements and stretching, and by bending and rotating the spinal column.

In every situation, our position on the horse is significantly influenced by the vestibular system.

SYSTEM 4: THE RESPIRATORY SYSTEM

"Practice breathing? Why? If I couldn't breathe, I wouldn't be here at all. I don't need to practice it, because I can already do it!"

That's more or less how clients respond when I start talking about breathing techniques. Breathing is so normal, such a casual, automatic movement, that we don't pay it any attention, but there are many things that can go wrong and cause problems.

The effects of incorrect breathing patterns are widespread, but we rarely identify our breathing patterns as a cause, or even as a factor that might be contributing to an existing problem.

Have you ever suffered from pneumonia, severe bronchitis, asthma, or other breathing difficulties? Have you ever bruised or broken your ribs? Do you have scars on your upper body? Do you occasionally hyperventilate? Do you have problems with anxiety or stress? Do you have problems with lymph flow? Are your vitamin D levels always low, despite taking supplements? Do you have problems concentrating? Do you have cold hands or cold feet—are you always wearing socks when you're sitting on the couch? Do you suffer from allergies, COPD, diabetes, or heart disease? Do you generally often feel very tired? Do you avoid any kind of intense cardiovascular activity? Do you sleep badly? Do you have high blood pressure? Do you still feel tired in the morning? Are you in pain? Do you have sore shoulders, a sore neck, back pain, or frequent cramps? Are you sensitive to bright lights or loud noises? Are your calcium levels low? Do you suffer from osteoporosis?

If you have answered "yes" to even one of these questions, I definitely advise you to do these drills. Do them often. Think back to the potential dangers the brain is constantly detecting. If you experience any of the problems listed above, training your breath can be the key to significantly reducing your brain's perception of danger, which will have a direct effect on your riding.

THE DIAPHRAGM—THE CENTER OF THE BODY

The diaphragm is the most important of our eight respiratory muscles. It's a special muscle that divides our upper body in two, like the mid-level floor in a two-story building. It attaches to the ribs and spine, and is normally examined in the context of general metabolic function. The diaphragm's important role in stabilizing our posture at rest and during movement—especially the rider's movement—is usually studiously

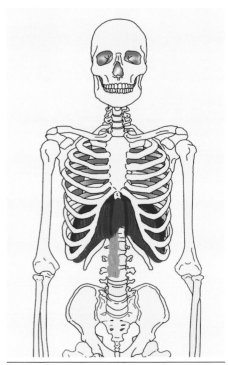

The diaphragm—a stabilizing muscle.

avoided (Hodges and Gandevia 2000; Kolar et al. 2012).

When you think about the central position of the diaphragm in the body and its vital function, it will soon become apparent that the diaphragm is a crucial muscle. Weightlifters have been making use of its stabilizing function for years. During the stretching phase, weightlifters will hold their breath, using what's known as the *Valsalva maneuver* to increase the pressure inside the stomach and chest, and therefore improve their stability and the quality of weight transfer and force generation. The diaphragm has fascial connections to the *costal pleura* and *pericardium*, as well as the *scalene muscles*, which help with rapid breathing in and laterally stabilize the head, the occipital bone, and the *dura mater* (outer meninges).

At the back, the diaphragm has fascial connections to the *psoas*—the lumbar flexor muscle. The diaphragm is also connected to the transverse abdominal muscles (*transversus abdominis*), the pubic bone, and the muscles of the pelvic floor. It therefore directly influences our posture through many different areas (González-Álvarez et al. 2016; Hodges and Gandevia 2000; Kolar et al. 2012; Kocjan et al. 2018).

ACTIVATING THE BRAIN THROUGH BREATHING

Voluntary breathing in the form of breathing training activates many areas of the brain, such as the frontal lobes, which are responsible for planning and decision-making as well as estimating the consequences of our actions. The supplementary motor area, which is responsible for preparing for movement, is involved in the bilateral movements that are important in riding.

Abdominal breathing against resistance = activated diaphragm.

Seated diaphragm stretch ...

... for better core stability and more oxygenated blood.

Voluntary breathing activates the *basal ganglia* that design the movement plan on behalf of the motor cortex and inhibit unwanted movement patterns. It also activates the insular cortex in the brain that produces feelings such as hunger, tiredness, or happiness, and is also responsible for adjustment and planning of use of strength, blood pressure and other capabilities in movement. Not forgetting the cerebellum that is constantly correcting errors for all movements and thoughts and adjusts the tension of the extensor muscles on each side of the body (Herrero et al. 2018).

FUEL FOR THE BRAIN

Our brain needs fuel and activation for healthy function. Conscious breathing achieves good activation in the aforementioned brain areas and promotes fuel supply—in the form of an even balance between oxygen and carbon dioxide. The latter admittedly isn't primarily a fuel, but it does some wonderful things in our body, one of which is ensure that adequate quantities of oxygen can reach the brain through dilated blood vessels—if present in an appropriate ratio to oxygen, and not in excessive amounts. My experience is that a good two-thirds of people will benefit from voluntary breathing in the form of breathing training. It might seem simple, but complicated solutions on a molecular or genetic level are not always required to solve big problems. It's very often small things over time that make a big difference in our lives—and because of its far-reaching biochemical, neuroanatomical, and anatomical casual networks, correct breathing is one of them. No other activities can be performed well without a good supply of oxygen to the brain. You'll find exercises for breathing starting on page 139.

PREPARING FOR NEURO-RIDER TRAINING

If you are or have been injured, and you're unsure as to whether you should do certain exercises, you should seek advice from a doctor you trust. You must seek medical advice if you have any of the problems listed below.

CAUTION! CONTRAINDICATIONS

— Joint hypermobility—especially following a ligament tear.
— Articular effusion (swelling)—whether as a result of trauma or illness.
— Inflammation—joint inflammation with heat, redness, and/or swelling.

— Tumors—many types of malignant tumors impair bone health and density.
— Diseases that weaken the bones—this can lead to breaks or injuries.
— Fractures—joint mobilizations are not suitable for parts of the body that have recently been fractured.

A strong correction puts an end to the balance test.

The left hip circle improves balance.

*"Never train
in pain!"*

Perfect execution always begins ...

— Total joint replacement—all movements should be cleared by a physician.
— Post-operative recovery—joint mobilizations can be inappropriate during the early recovery phase.

SUCCESS IS DIFFICULT WITHOUT A GOAL

Our brains struggle without goals to orient them. They don't have any direction and don't know what's important to us. If you don't know what your goal is, don't be surprised if you end up somewhere you don't want to be. We shouldn't underestimate the importance of goal setting, and of finding straightforward ways to state our goals for ourselves. Most riders don't have a clear goal for their sessions, but if you want to improve, more focus can be helpful. You should set a goal you want to work towards for certain sessions. How to set goals well is a topic that could fill books, but here are some ways to approach the problem of setting a goal for your training! Take a few minutes' time and consider:

— What do you specifically want to improve?
— When do you want to achieve this?
— Is your goal measurable? (If it isn't, then make it measurable.)
— Can you use video to compare "before" with "after"?

— If your goal is to have more fun—then ask yourself: "How much fun have I been having so far, on a scale of 1 to 10?" What is your average fun factor? What would have to happen to improve your fun factor by one point?
— Is the goal really important to you? Is it attractive enough?
— Can you visualize achieving your goal? Can you state it clearly? Write it down— copy it onto multiple sticky notes and put them somewhere you'll see them, as reminders for your training.

... with a neutral standing position (see p. 70).

(see p. 70)

MASTERFUL MOVEMENT
— Make sure you execute the movements perfectly.
— Correct your posture; when possible, always keep your spine long and tall.
— Synchronize your breathing with the movement.
— Only tense your muscles if you really need to for the movement.
— Caution: If you do an exercise in an imperfect posture, you'll get better at doing the exercise in an imperfect posture, and we don't want that.
— If you do any exercises with excessive muscle tension in parts of the body that aren't involved in the exercise, you'll get better at producing excessive muscle tension. You'll train yourself to have tension, be slow, and be in more pain. So always be very focused, and pay attention when executing the exercises. Think about top athletes who always make everything look easy. But how do you achieve masterful movement?

PERFECT EXECUTION

Here's a perspective that 35-time pole-vault world record holder Sergey Bubka shared with my former colleague Dr. Christian Uhl years ago. When asked about the secret to his success, Bubka said:

"After my initial successes, I lost focus and concentrated too much on things that weren't important. I noticed my mistakes and started to work on the basics of my sport again: precise movement, basic running technique. I trained the fundamentals that nine-year-olds would normally learn to bring my basics up to a higher level. Tall towers can only be built on good foundations. My training mostly consists of basic training."

The foundations of effective movement are the perfect function of the visual, vestibular, and proprioceptive systems. We are working on these foundations. And when we do that, we must pay attention to the following points so we practice the basics the right way.

TARGET THE RIGHT AREA

Always focus precisely on the area or detail given as the focal point of the drill. Ignore everything else you feel when doing the drill. When you are learning and performing the drill, it's very important for you to keep reflecting and checking on what you're doing when you move.

SLOW MOTION OR HIGH SPEED?

The speed at which we do an exercise makes a difference. However, that doesn't mean moving fast is bad. It often takes more speed to achieve enough activation to make a change. Nevertheless, I recommend starting with slow movements (see the slow area of the diagram below).

On the other hand, stimuli that are new to us can often be extremely effective, whether fast or slow. Try to keep to the time frame for every exercise. "Slow" means you should take at least five to ten seconds for a single repetition. Five to ten seconds gives you the chance to direct your focus and your full attention onto the right area of movement. Practice that first. You should also remember that different speeds affect different groups of receptors. Other speeds can achieve completely different effects.

This means an exercise performed at a slow speed might only have a small effect in relation to your goal but doing the same exercise fast might be a magic bullet for you. So remember to play around with different training speeds as soon as you've mastered an exercise in perfect form.

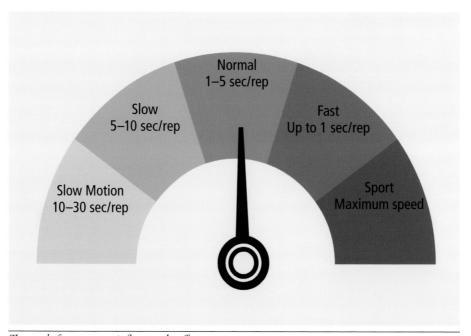

The speed of a movement influences the effect.

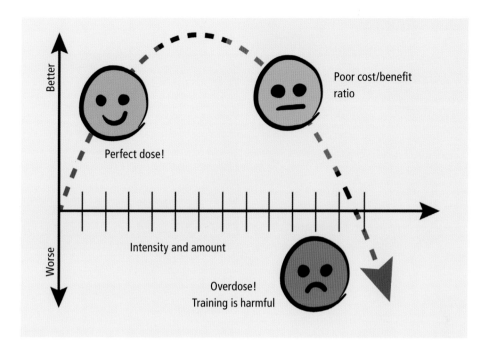

THE DOSE MAKES THE MEDICINE

Training is like medication. And you can absolutely cause yourself harm with training, just like you can cause yourself harm by overdosing on a medicine that would have cured you in a smaller amount. Many people don't think enough about this fact.

Find the right dose for you and choose the minimum effective dose (see green area). Unless you're bored—but you shouldn't be, because you're riding!

STOP WHEN IT FEELS GOOD

There is another motivational reason for this: If your training is always too hard and strenuous, and you feel worse after doing it than you did before, your nervous system will remember this, and you will feel less enthusiastic about repeating training. On the other hand, if you stop when training feels its best, if you've achieved a lot of benefit at little cost, that's a good time to stop training. Improving performance with the minimum effective dose and feeling better after training than you did before is a nice reward. And behavioral research shows that rewards are necessary to form a habit!

ALWAYS FEEL THE MOVEMENT

This principle is very easy to put into practice. You activate precisely the area that you want to move—for example, by rubbing it with gentle or firm pressure, by tapping the area, or by applying vibration using a vibration tool. Focus on what you feel! You can also activate a body part while watching TV, but it'll have less effect on your brain than activation before executing a drill, and it'll also be less beneficial to your movement.

1

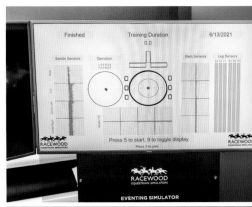

2

3

4

1 – 5   *Sensors measure seat and effectiveness in different situations on the riding simulator nicknamed "Sir Waldo." This is a good opportunity to improve the rider's actions with targeted training stimuli and to look at the results immediately, before switching to a real horse.*

5

Based on an understanding of anatomy and blood supply, we can work on the following assumption when it comes to fundamental brain activity patterns: *Activation happens from the bottom up and from back to front.* In order for the motor cortex to be able to send good signals to the muscles, it's useful to pre-activate the sensory cortex in the parietal lobes—because if we're "warmed up" there, and blood circulation is increased, the motor cortex has better conditions to work in.

FUEL AND ACTIVATION

Neuroplasticity—learning—is successful if two prerequisites are met: *fuel* and *activation.*

The drills I present starting on page 47 result in activation. However, activation alone, without enough fuel, will cause problems sooner or later. It's like driving a car: With no oil in the engine, going from a cold start to full throttle only results in piston seizure.

The brain doesn't need oil, but it does need oxygen and glucose. We take care of oxygen supply with the exercises in the chapter on breathing (p. 139). The brain is an outstanding internal combustion engine for sugar. It uses up around one-third of your carbohydrate intake, even though it only weighs two and a half pounds! Amazing, isn't it? However, this means that if you don't eat enough carbohydrates, and your brain doesn't get enough sugar, the metabolic situation in your brain will suffer—and so will its function.

When we learn something new, which you will as soon as you begin training, your brain will start needing more glucose. The eye exercises and the drills for the vestibular system are particularly demanding for your brain. Please make sure that you start your training with breathing exercises and, ideally, a glass of orange juice.

Your brain will run into problems without fuel.

THE FOUNDATION —
Testing and Retesting

THE PRINCIPLE: TEST— DRILL—RETEST

In neuroathletic training, you test your mobility, balance and coordination and differences in laterality. Then you do the drills and test again.

TEST YOURSELF

What happens when a car horn sounds right next to you? You jump. What happens when you watch a tense thriller? Your palms become sweaty, and your heart rate accelerates. What sometimes happens when someone gives you a compliment? You blush.

The nervous system is constantly reacting to what's happening in and around us. These instant effects are all too familiar. Let's start using the nervous system's rapid responses to find out which training stimuli elicit a positive response in the brain, and which it categorizes as threatening. When our nervous system enables more flexibility, balance, or coordination, then we can categorize the stimulus that caused it as positive. If our flexibility, balance, or coordination are worse after a training drill, then the brain has categorized this stimulus as potentially threatening.

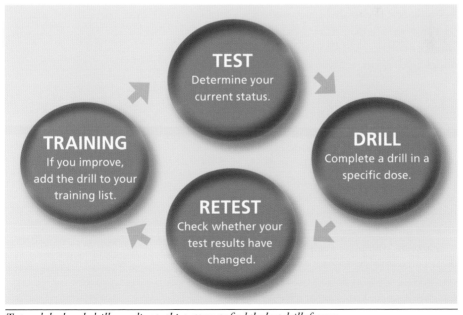

Test and check each drill according to this pattern to find the best drills for you.

CHANGES WITH BRAIN SPEED

One basic rule is: changes happen fast—at the speed of the nervous system. Remember how our brain works. It's always doing three things: receiving input; interpreting that input and making decisions; and producing output (see p. 17). A nerve signal travels along a nerve fiber at speeds of between around 0.5 and 12 meters per second (1.5 to almost 40 feet per second), depending on the type of fiber. So when you do a drill, the brain responds to it almost immediately. This response can be a protective response that causes your flexibility, balance, or coordination to deteriorate.

However, your brain might also enjoy the stimulus generated by the drill and respond by improving flexibility, balance, and coordination. Drills can be effective for different lengths of time. It depends on how

the drill is performed and on the person performing the drill. We can be relatively certain the effect will still be noticeable in the retest after 10 to 30 seconds. For that reason, you should do retests right after doing a drill.

TESTS FOR TRAINING AT HOME

The Neuro-Rider Training begins in this chapter. I'll describe the tests you can use that have proven to be beneficial for equestrians. Please familiarize yourself with the tests and read through the descriptions several times. You should do the tests precisely and in the same way each time. Take your time. Find out which tests are suitable for you, establish differences between each side of the body if relevant, and record the results in the table. Copy the table so you can enter test results more than once. Use your smartphone to film yourself as you do the tests, to help you see the differences. (Before you begin, take a look at the FAN information on page 149.)

Be your biggest FAN (see p. 149).

TESTING THE DRILLS

Take a little time for the next step. Don't make the mistake of testing all the drills one after another on the same day. You'll be able to do so after a few weeks, but not at first. When you're just starting out, speed comes at the expense of quality of execution. Take enough time to pay attention to and meet all the requirements for execution. I describe 62 drills in this book. Later, you won't always have to repeat all the tests or check every drill with all the tests—you can pick and choose. As a horseback rider, it makes sense to choose a balance test—for example, a difficult Zombie Stand or Walk the Line (see pp. 56 and 59). Full Body Rotation and the Forward Bend (see pp. 54 and 51) have also proven to be useful to many people. Test what's important for you!

Test and Retest	On Side	Distance	Reduced Left	Reduced Right	Fall Direction Tendency	Standing Time	Pain 0–10	Other Observations
Flexibility								
Forward Bend	51							
Scarecrow Inward Rotation	52							
Scarecrow Outward Rotation	52							
Half Snow Angel	53							
Shoulder Flexion	54							
Pistol Rotation	54							
Balance								
Zombie Stand	56							
Intensified Zombie Stand	57							
One-Legged Zombie Stand with Knee Raise	58							
Walk the Line	59							
Coordination								
Hand RAPS	59							

This is a universal tracking table: not all columns are relevant for every test.

FLEXIBILITY TESTS

Flexibility tests are a general test of the flexibility of different areas of your body. You'll find out what range of motion your brain currently allows, and whether there are differences between the two sides of your body. Repeat the tests a few times in a row, until you've developed a good feel for your current capacity.

FORWARD BEND

HIP FLEXION

Focus on: How far can I bend when I'm relaxed? How do my muscles feel when I stretch? Tense? Relaxed? How far are my fingertips from the floor? How much of my hand can I put on the floor?

How to do it: Stand up straight with your spine long and tall, your feet shoulder-width apart, and your toes pointing forwards. Now bend your upper body forward and let your arms hang down, with your fingertips pointing to the tips of your toes. Allow yourself to relax and hang down, and notice how big the distance between your fingertips and your toes is. Don't bob up and down, and don't force yourself down. Just let your upper body hang. Notice where your muscles and tendons are tense. Notice the distance from your fingers to the floor and how easy or difficult you find this position. You should repeat the process several times in a row to begin with, as a warmup. Otherwise, it wouldn't be surprising if you did better in the retest, simply because the test had loosened things up a little.

Just allow yourself to relax and hang down.

Feel free to repeat the forward bend several times.

SCARECROW

INWARD AND OUTWARD SHOULDER ROTATION

Focus on: How far can I rotate? How easy or difficult is it? Is one side weaker? Do this test with both shoulders and compare each side. Are there differences in your range of movement? Which positions can you achieve on which side? Take note of the most restricted position and repeat it later in the retest!

How to do it: Stand up straight with your spine long and tall, your feet shoulder-width apart, and your toes pointing forward. Look straight ahead and focus on an object or point in front of you. Raise your right arm horizontally to the side, and bend your elbow so your forearm is at a right angle to your upper arm. Your palm should be facing the floor. Your upper arm should be horizontal for the whole exercise. Now rotate your shoulder so the back of your hand moves up and back. How far can you rotate your shoulder?

Outward rotation.

Inward rotation.

Take note of your biggest possible movement radius/the point at which you feel you can't move your hand up and back any further.

Now rotate your shoulder forward and down, and move your palm down until it faces backward. How far can you rotate your shoulder like that? Take note of your biggest possible movement radius. If you can rotate further but feel pain in your shoulder when you do, then the point up to which you can move without pain is your result.

HALF SNOW ANGEL

SHOULDER ABDUCTION

Focus on: How far can I rotate? How easy or difficult is it? Is one side weaker? Do this test with both shoulders and compare each side. Are there differences in the range of movement? Which shoulder has a smaller range of movement, and which shoulder moves less "fluidly"? Test both sides and take note of any differences. However, we are again mainly interested in the worse side, which we'll test again during the retest to check how effective the drill has been.

How to do it: Stand up straight with your spine long and tall, your feet shoulder-width apart, and your toes pointing forwards. Look straight ahead and focus on an object or point in front of you. Keeping your right arm completely straight, raise it as high as possible next to your body. Observe the range of movement and how easy or difficult you find the movement. It would be perfect if your upper arm touched your ear at the end of the movement—but don't move your ear toward your arm! If you can reach farther but feel pain in your shoulder when you do, then the point up to which you can move without pain is your result.

Maximum movement range in flexion.

Raise your arm in front of you.   *Stretch your arm.*   *Keep your upper body still.*

SHOULDER FLEXION

Focus on: How far can I raise my stretched arm in the correct position? How easy or difficult is it? Is one side weaker? How do my shoulders feel? Do this test with both shoulders and compare each side.

How to do it: Stand up straight with your spine long and tall, your feet shoulder-width apart, and your toes pointing forward. Look straight ahead and focus on an object or point in front of you. Keeping your right arm completely straight at the elbow, raise it in front of you, and move it as high up as possible. Make sure you keep your elbow completely straight the whole time. It would be perfect if your upper arm touched your ear at the end of the movement. Take note of your maximum range of motion and observe how easy or difficult you find the movement. Test both sides and observe any differences. Establish which side is your weaker side and retest it. If you can reach farther but feel pain in your shoulder when you do, then the point up to which you can move without pain is your result.

PISTOL ROTATION

FULL BODY ROTATION

Focus on: How far can I rotate? How easy or difficult is it? Is there a weaker side where I can't rotate as far? How securely do I stand during the exercise?

How to do it: Stand with your feet close together and your ankles touching. Stand up straight, with your spine long and tall. Stretch your arms horizontally in front of you and hold your hands as if you were aiming a gun straight in front of you.

Keep your elbows completely straight. Now turn your whole body as far as possible to the left, and take note of the final position you can reach. Come back to the center, and then rotate to the right. Again, see how far you can rotate.

You can pick specific points in the room and aim at them. Repeat these rotations a few times until you have established where your maximum rotation range is and to which side you are less able to rotate. Take note of the results.

When you do a retest for this test, it's a good idea to stand in exactly the same place you stood the first time, so you can use the

BALANCE TESTS

Focus on: How secure do I feel? How much do I wobble? How long can I stand stably without having to move to regain my balance?

The balance tests give you two pieces of information: firstly, how good your physical awareness (proprioception) is, and secondly, how reliably the vestibular system in your inner ear works. Sometimes your first attempt at standing will be a complete flop, so feel free to do two or three attempts to get a good feel for your current capacity.

Later in training, you'll only need to do one of the balance tests. Choose a level of difficulty you find challenging. If you can stand in a normal Zombie Stand with your eyes closed for 20 seconds without swaying too much, then it's too easy, and you won't be able to tell whether you're improving. Choose a test where you can build on your performance!

Around to the right.

Stretch your elbows.

Around to the left.

same fixed points to measure your range of rotation. We want to improve rotation to the weaker side in the retest.

Don't move into pain. If you feel pain, then the point up to which you can move without pain is your result. Repeat the rotations a few times until you have warmed up.

ZOMBIE STAND

Caution: Make sure there aren't any sharp objects around you. If you have balance problems, do this test standing in the corner of a room with your back to the wall, so you have the corner close behind you and the walls to your right and left.

How to do it: Stand with your feet close together and your ankles touching. Stand up straight, with your spine long and tall. Stretch your arms out horizontally in front of you. Stretch your elbows and your fingers. Observe whether your body sways forward and back or left and right. Now close your eyes. Notice whether your body sways for-

1

1 *Feet together.*
2 *Arms stretched out horizontally.*
3 *Eyes closed.*

2

3

2   *3*   *4*

1   *5*

1 Intensified Zombie Stand.
2 Toe behind the heel.
3 Test both sides.
4 Slightly easier: feet offset.
5 One foot's length of distance.

ward and back or left and right.

Feel whether your body prefers to sway in one direction. As soon as you need to move your arms or upper body to correct yourself, that's the end of the test. Take note of how long you could stand until you needed to stop.

Take it as a positive sign if you can stand more securely during the retest, or if you stop swaying to one side. If you don't wobble at all during the zombie stand, then this test is too easy for you—use the intensified zombie stand.

INTENSIFIED ZOMBIE STAND

How to do it: Identical to the Zombie Stand, but your feet are not side by side; instead, put them one behind the other, with the toes of your right foot touching the heel of your left foot. Your weight should be evenly distributed across both feet. You should also test the position with your right foot forward. If you find yourself too wobbly, you can make this test easier by not standing with your feet in line, but rather slightly apart. Can you manage both solidly, as if your feet were sunk into concrete? Then try the One-Legged Zombie Stand. As we've already said, find a standing position that feels secure but also challenging; that way, you'll be able to tell when you're improving.

1

2

3

4

1 *One-Legged Zombie Stand with the eyes open.*
2 *One-Legged Zombie Stand with the eyes closed.*
3 *The right side is wobblier!*
4 *The test is over if you need to make big compensatory movements with your upper body and take your arms out of the "zombie position" to stop yourself from falling over.*

ONE-LEGGED ZOMBIE STAND

How to do it: Stand up straight and stable with your eyes open. Lift one foot off the floor, and raise your thigh—hold your bent leg in this position until you've found your balance. If you can stand stable like this without making any corrections with your arms or hips, you can also close your eyes.

Count the seconds until you need to make a big corrective movement. Compensatory movements in the ankles are completely normal. Repeat the One-Legged Zombie Stand three times on each leg. Add up the seconds of all three attempts. Divide the total by three to give you your average baseline. Establish whether there are differences between standing on your right and left leg. You should also note how high you can raise your right thigh compared with your left thigh.

WALK THE LINE

How to do it: For guidance you will need a straight line on the ground, 10 to 15 feet (3 to 5 meters) long. Mark one with chalk or tape, or place a lunge line on the ground. Stand in the intensified zombie stand at the start of the line, and then walk slowly and precisely along the line, touching the heel of your front foot directly to the toe of your back foot. Notice which direction you tend to tip, or in which direction you tend to feel pulled.

1   2   3

1 Can you walk straight ...
2 ... with your eyes closed ...
3 ... along the line?

HAND RAPS

(Rapid Alternating Pronation and Supination)

Focus on: Which side is weaker, slower, and less rhythmical? That's the side on which the cerebellum works less well, and therefore the side you should use as a test and retest.

That means paying attention to whether your weaker side gets better at the Hand

Hand RAPS: Clapping...

... with the palm and the back of the hand.

Fast and rhythmical.

RAPS after training. If yes, then you've found a drill that can help you.

How to do it: Hold your left hand in front of you around belly button height, with your fingers straight and your palm facing up. Now clap the *palm* of your right hand against the palm of your left hand. Then, quickly turn your hands and clap the *back* of your right hand against your left palm; turn them quickly again and clap the palms, and continue like this, alternating between the back of your right hand and the palm. The edges of your hands mustn't touch during the transition. Do as many claps as you can in five seconds. Pay attention to the speed and rhythm of your clapping.

Now swap hands so the left hand is clapping against the right hand, quickly alternating between the palm and the back of the left hand. Again, do as many claps as you can, as rhythmically as you can, in five seconds.

It's enough to do this test for five seconds at maximum speed and in the best possible rhythm.

COORDINATION

Hand RAPS test the function of the cerebellum. The cerebellum is responsible for accurate movements, rhythm, balance, and coordination. Here, the abbreviation "RAPS" doesn't have anything to do with "rapping" in a musical sense. RAPS stands for "Rapid Alternating Pronation and Supination," which in this case refers to turning the forearms and hand up and down.

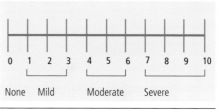

1 *"How painful was it?"*
2 *Data collection with scales is useful for documenting progress.*
3 *The numerical pain scale.*

1

3

PAIN

If your goal is to reduce pain, then you need to be able to measure it first; use a *pain scale*. Enter your current level of pain, and then the worst pain and the least pain you've experienced in the last 24 hours, on a scale of 0 = no pain to 10 = the worst pain imaginable. Measure your pain against this scale every day and note it somewhere, so you're documenting any change over a longer period. This will enable you to directly assess the effect of your training and the effect of each drill, both before and after training, and after each individual drill that you do.

You should obviously only train the drills that reduce your pain.

TEST OTHER MOVEMENTS

It goes without saying that you can use other movements as tests and retests, not just the ones described here. You need to make sure the test conditions are easy to standardize, and the movements shouldn't be influenced by too many factors.

For example, in my work with clients, I use their gait pattern as a test and retest opportunity. It's a completely valid test of autonomous movement where you can largely switch off cognitive influence with additional exercises. However, it takes a little practice, and you need to know what to look for.

There are many ways to test the effect of input stimuli on the nervous system: walking down stairs, getting up from a chair, shooting precision and strength in soccer, a one-legged deep lunge, a pull-up, your own handwriting, playing a tune on an instrument, changes in visual acuity, changes in olfactory perception or in intensity of perception of touch, the ability to perceive taste, or data such as blood pressure, pulse rate, or body temperature.

More like this: a "Power Drill."

CATEGORIZATION OF DRILLS: POWER–REHAB–NEUTRAL

We divide up drills into three categories based on the results they deliver.

Power Drill	Rehab Drill	Neutral Drill
A drill that improves one or several retests.	A drill that makes one or several retests worse.	A drill that makes you neither better nor worse.
Your nervous system responds positively and is "happy."	Your nervous system responds with protective reactions.	Your nervous system can satisfy the requirements for this drill very well. The processing of the stimuli signals works well!
You can incorporate these stimuli into every training session and play with the dosage. Do as many of them as you can.	Don't train with these drills. "Rehab" comes from "rehabilitation." There are no movements and no stimuli in this book to which your brain should have to respond with protective reactions. As your training progresses you should rehabilitate these stimuli.	Try to increase the number of repetitions a little and then retest. Neutral Drills are useful and important, because we can use them later, together with the Power Drills, to rehabilitate the Rehab Drills.

I didn't like it, but it was still good. *Good: a Neutral Drill.* *Rehab Drill: There's work to do.*

I DIDN'T LIKE IT, BUT IT WAS STILL GOOD!

And then there's a fourth category: You will find that there are drills you don't like. These are often drills you find difficult. That doesn't matter. If you retest positively after doing these drills, then they're Power Drills and they'll make you better! There will also be drills you find easier, but that have a neutral or even negative retest result.

THE TEST IS PART OF THE TRAINING

If you keep repeating a test, then obviously you'll improve. If you repeat a test enough times, then at some point, that test will lose its ability to deliver valid data about your brain function. But that isn't all bad: If the act of testing improves your ability to do the test movement, the test has become therapy, and repeated therapy has become training.

Let's take an example: If I do squats with 110 pounds of weight as a test, repeat the test several times a day for three weeks, and then manage 130 pounds, have I ruined the test? Not at all—I would actually call that successful training! Repeated testing = therapy = training. If you feel that a test is losing its meaning, then it's time to change the test or make it more demanding.

"Don't fall into the trap of only training the drills you like. Train the drills that make you better!"

63

NEURO-RIDER
MOVEMENTS
— *Let's Go!*

PHYSICAL AWARENESS OR PROPRIOCEPTION

The following applies to all Neuro-Rider Movements: To begin with, start the exercise in a neutral stance with your spine straight, regardless of whether you are doing the drills to improve your physical awareness, sight, balance, or respiratory system.

TRAINING YOUR PHYSICAL AWARENESS

The best way to develop better physical awareness is to control individual joints very precisely, and learn to move them through their full range of movement. We begin with structures at the center of the body before turning to the exercises for the joints of the extremities.

TONGUE MOVEMENTS

Tongue drills are among my absolute favorite exercises. They're very easy to learn and extremely effective, in both the short and long term. You don't need to put in a lot of effort to achieve a big effect. Tongue drills are particularly well-suited to riders because they activate the central cerebellum that is responsible for things like correcting the movements of the spine and eye muscles. Tongue drills also act on the supplementary motor area, an area of the brain involved in preparation for bilateral movement patterns (Scoppa et al. 2020).

But that's not all. From a neuronal point of view, the tongue is a very important interface between an organism and its environment. We take in food and fluids through the mouth. From an evolutionary perspective, it therefore makes sense that our nervous system has positioned some very finely tuned security checks in our mouths. Scientists all over the world have recognized the importance of the tongue as the "gateway to the brain," and there are many interesting approaches and exercises

How much strength does the tongue have?

65

involving the tongue in neural retraining and for rehabilitation after traumatic injuries or illnesses.

Numerous studies show that activating the tongue aids neuroplastic processes and learning. That means that by doing tongue drills before you ride, you can improve your chances of quick and lasting learning.

HOW DOES IT WORK?

The following applies to all parts of the exercise: As mentioned, start the exercise in a neutral position with your spine straight.

First learn how to get into a perfect ...

Step 1	Read the description of the first drill.
Step 2	Do your favorite test.
Step 3	Do the first drill as described.
Step 4	Re-test Step 2.
Step 5	Mark the table under NEUTRAL, REHAB, or POWER, depending on what kind of drill it is according to your test result.
Step 6	Repeat steps 1 to 5 for the second drill.
Step 7	Repeat steps 1 to 5 for the third drill.
...	
...	
Step "n"	Repeat steps 1 to 5 for the "nth" drill.

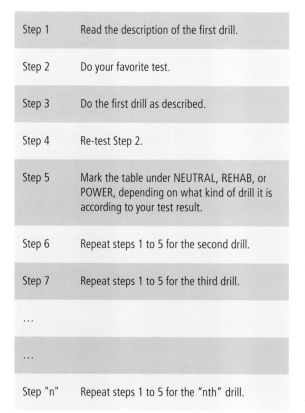

... neutral standing position (see p. 70).

Tests and Drills Physical Awareness— Proprioception	On page	Result, Left Side			Result, Right Side		
		Neutral	Rehab	Power	Neutral	Rehab	Power
Tongue in Resting Position, Fake Smile, and Swallow	68						
Tongue Circles with the Mouth Closed	68						
Press the Tongue into Right and Left Cheek	68						
Tongue Stretch	69						
Vibration on the Teeth	70						
Neutral Standing Position with the Spine Long	70						
Push the Head Forward	72						
Push the Head Back	74						
Push the Head Left	74						
Push the Head Right	75						
Half No	76						
Yes-Yes Movement	78						
Lateral Bend of the Cervical Vertebrae	79						
The Hen	80						
The Pecking Hen	80						
The Hen in Sideways Position	82						
Bend and Stretch the Thoracic Spine	83						
Thoracic Spine in Sideways Position	85						
Lumbar Spine in Semicircle Forward	86						
Lumbar spine in Semicircle Backward	88						
Straighten and Tilt Pelvis	89						
Pelvic Rotations	90						
Figure Eights with the Hands	91						
Forward Shoulder Circles	92						
Cross-Body Shoulder Circles	92						
Sideways Shoulder Circles	93						
Forward Hip Circles	94						
Cross-Body Hip Circles	96						
Sideways Hip Circles	96						
Backward Hip Circles	96						
Knee Circles	97						
Tilt Ankle Outward	98						
Tilt Ankle Inward	98						
Pull Toes Straight	99						
Pull Toes Out	100						
Isometric Full-Body Contraction	100						

Tip of the tongue behind the incisors ...

... then swallow and "smile."

TONGUE IN RESTING POSITION, FAKE SMILE, AND SWALLOW

Focus on: Contact surface of tongue on palate—pay attention to the pressure.

How to do it:
— Try a test.
— Place the tip of your tongue behind the incisors on your upper palate, and swallow. Breathe out slowly through your nose. Your tongue will now be in the physiological resting position, against the palate.

— Leaving your tongue where it is, start to grin broadly. Breathe in for two seconds and hold this "fake smile" face; then swallow and breathe out slowly through your nose. Hold the grin and swallow five times in a row. A sip of water will help if your mouth gets too dry.
— Retest, and record the result in the table.

TONGUE CIRCLES WITH THE MOUTH CLOSED

Focus on: Feel on the tongue—even movement.

How to do it:
— Try a test.
— Run the tip of your tongue over the outside edge of your incisors and molars, so you're making the biggest circle possible in your mouth with your tongue.
— As a preparatory or intensification drill: repeat this movement for approximately 30 seconds to a minute. Change direction!
— Retest, and record the result in the table.

PRESS THE TONGUE INTO THE RIGHT AND LEFT CHEEK

Focus on: Even force generation in the root of the tongue.

How to do it:
— Try a test.
— Press your tongue into your right cheek as firmly as possible, with consistent pressure. You can use your hand to exert slight counterpressure from the outside. As a preparatory or intensification drill: repeat for approximately 30 seconds to a minute.
— Retest, and record the result in the table.

During the tongue circles you can ...

.. feel your tongue stretching.

Try to make the circle as even ...

... and as big as possible.

— Repeat the drill, pressing your tongue into your left cheek.
— Retest a second time, and record the result in the table.

TONGUE STRETCH

Focus on: Generate even pressure, feel a slight stretch.

How to do it:
— Try a test.
— Roll your tongue so the underside of the tip of your tongue touches your palate. Now try to bring as much of the underside of your tongue as possible into contact with your palate and press the underside of your tongue firmly against your palate. Hold this position for 30 seconds to a minute.

Retest, and record the result in the table.

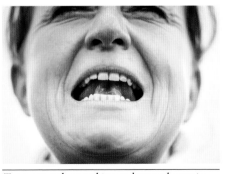

Tongue stretch: stretching and strength exercise.

Test the vibration on your incisors, ...

... bite with your right molars, ...

... and then bite with your left molars.

NEUTRAL STANDING POSITION

Learn to control and mobilize your spine. This drill should be at the top of your list of exercises. You might be wondering why. The neutral standing position with the spine long might just be the most important but most underestimated exercise in the world—perhaps because it seems so trivial, ordinary, and simple.

VIBRATION ON THE TEETH

Focus on: The vibration.

How to do it:

— Try a test.

— Take a disposable electric toothbrush without the brush attachment, or a Z-Vibe tool (a vibratory oral motor tool), and put it into your mouth; start the vibration, and then bite down gently on the shaft with your incisors. You can change position after 10 seconds, and use your molars to bite down onto the tool, on one side and then the other. As you do so, explore where you can feel the vibration the most on your tongue. The stimulation should last for at least a minute.

— Retest, and record the result in the table.

NEUTRAL STANDING POSITION WITH THE SPINE LONG

People often react to Neutral Standing Position the same way they react to the idea of breathing exercises: "Standing up straight? What's the big deal?" Being able to do something at all and being able to do it efficiently with excellence are two different things. We're working on achieving outstanding movement quality for the most essential functions of our bodies. And if we improve the way we engage in these basic functions, it has a positive effect on all other associated functions.

The Neutral Standing Position is the starting position for almost all other exercises, and will become—please, please, please—your new basic position. If you can learn to hold your head on a neutral axis, you will reduce excess muscle tension and improve your muscular balance. You can practice the neutral standing position anywhere and everywhere: in the shower, waiting in line at the supermarket, at a party, anywhere you are standing.

So what are you waiting for?

Focus on: To create as much distance as possible between your pelvic floor and the back "points of the crown" that you imagine wearing on your head.

How to do it:
— Try a test. (Please *always* do the following steps in the sequence described.)
— Stand with your feet shoulder-width apart.
— Bend your knees slightly and keep them in that slightly bent position. Now straighten your pelvis—imagine the movement a dog makes when it tucks its tail between its legs. Or you can also imagine you want to subtly check and

make sure your fly is closed! When your "tail is tucked in"—your pelvis is straight—then bring your spine into the vertical position: first the bottom part (the lumbar spine), then the middle part (the thoracic spine), and finally the upper (cervical spine).
— To finish, position your chin slightly down and back toward your Adam's apple so you can feel your cervical spine flex slightly at the nape of your neck. Have you got everything in order? Good!
— Then slowly fully extend your knee joints and use your legs to push your body up like a hydraulic lift. Make sure your pelvis remains in its upright position. Actively push yourself further up. Imagine you're wearing a crown on your head, and you want to pierce a hole in the ceiling with the back point.

Neutral Standing Position: Bend your knees, straighten your pelvis, ...

... tuck your chin into your larynx, slowly straighten your knees, ...

... and then "push the points of your crown through the ceiling."

Remain in this extremely active, but motionless position for 20 to 40 seconds. As you do so, breathe in and out through your nose, steady and relaxed. If you can maintain the breathing rhythm—breathe in for two seconds, hold your breath for two seconds, breathe out for two seconds—it works out at two to four breaths (each breath lasts 10 seconds).
— Retest, and record the result in the table.

ISOMETRIC MUSCLE CONTRACTION

Isometric muscle contractions are simple, but extremely valuable drills. *Isometry* means "muscle contraction without movement." Isometric training has many effects.

— It lowers blood pressure.
— It's good for pain relief.
— You can use it to build muscle.
— It can make you stronger.
— It helps with fibromyalgia.
— Isometric neck training reduces the impacts of concussions. It might sound crazy, but if your neck muscles are trained, your head won't be flung back and forth as much after an impact. Makes sense, doesn't it?

For a very long time, I've been specifically using *isometric training* in performance sports to train certain kinds of movements when there has been a lack of strength development or abnormal movement.

Fascinatingly, the muscles of the neck have a direct neuronal connection to the vestibular system, namely via the nuclear complex of the vestibular system, the vestibular nuclei (*nucleus vestibularis*). Isometric muscle contractions therefore indirectly activate the vestibular system. This can be very helpful.

In our training, isometric contractions help firstly by strengthening the neck musculature and thereby helping us avoid concussions or reduce their severity. Secondly, they're ideal for activating the neck muscles, which are rarely used in everyday life. The following exercises for the cervical spine are rather delicate and geared towards precise motor controls. You'll learn to feel when you are doing them correctly, and you'll be able to do them better and better.

PUSH THE HEAD FORWARD

Focus on: Consistent tension in the muscles that rotate the head, the *sternocleidomastoid muscles*, which tense when you press to the right and left of your throat.

How to do it:
— Try a test.
— Rub the front of your neck with your hands for around 20 seconds, so you can really feel it. Stand in a neutral position (p. 70). Put one hand on top of the other and hold them in front of your forehead. Now push your forehead forward as if you were going to nod, and at the same time, push back with your hands against your forehead. Your head should stay still.

NECK ISOMETRY IN FOUR POSITIONS

Test every position separately—front, back, left and right. It could well be that you benefit from one direction in particular. Neck isometry is very good preparation for all elements of vestibular training (p. 127).

Don't push with all your strength; make sure you still feel as if you could press harder. Hold the contraction for eight to ten seconds. Relax the muscles as soon as possible after the exercise. Keep your breathing relaxed, and breathe in and out through your nose. This note about relaxed nasal breathing isn't an afterthought; it's important for the successful execution of this drill.

Retest, and record the result in the table.

1

2

3

4

5

1 First rub your neck, including the sides.

2 Rubbing will allow you to feel the muscles better.

3 A better feel for the muscles will make them easier to contract.

4 Push your head forward into your hands.

5 Push firmly, but not with your full strength: 8 to 10 seconds.

Push your head back.

Hold the contraction for 8 to 10 seconds.

PUSH THE HEAD BACK

Focus on: Consistent tension in the neck musculature.

How to do it:
— Try a test.
— Rub your neck with your hands for around 20 seconds. Stand in a neutral position (page 70). Clasp your hands and place them on the back of your head. You might be able to feel the muscles that start at your skull on the back of

your head. You should avoid touching them if possible. Push the back of your head back into your hands, as if you wanted to move your head to look above you, but don't actually look up. Don't push with all your strength; make sure you still feel as if you could push harder. Keep your breathing relaxed, and breathe in and out through your nose. Hold the contraction for eight to ten seconds.
— Retest, and record the result in the table.

PUSH THE HEAD TO THE LEFT

Focus on: Consistent tension in the left neck musculature.

How to do it:
— Try a test.
— Rub the left side of your neck with your hand for around 20 seconds. Stand in a neutral position. Place your left hand on the left side of your skull such that the ball of your hand is around two fingers' width above your auditory canal, and your fingers are pointing to the middle of your skull at the back.

First, rub your neck ...

Sensory activation through rubbing.

Motor activation through contraction.

Angle your left elbow out sideways so it points away from your body. Now push your head to the left, into your hand, and push back against it with your hand. Don't move your head. Don't push with all your strength; make sure you still feel as if you could push harder. Keep your breathing relaxed and breathe through your nose. Hold the contraction for eight to ten seconds.

Retest, and record the result in the table.

... then press your head into your hand.

PUSH THE HEAD TO THE RIGHT

Focus on: Consistent tension in the right neck musculature.

How to do it:
— Try a test.
— Rub the right side of your neck with your hand for around 20 seconds. Stand in a neutral position. Place your right hand on the right side of your skull, such that the ball of your hand is around two fingers' width above your auditory canal, and your fingers are pointing to the middle of your skull at the back. Angle your elbow out to the side so it points to the right, away from your body.
— Now push your head to the right into your hand, and push back against it with your hand. Don't move your head. Don't push with all your strength; make sure you still feel as if you could press harder. Keep your breathing relaxed and keep breathing through your nose. Hold the contraction for 8 to 10 seconds.
— Retest, and record the result in the table.

1

HALF NO

ROTATION OF THE CERVICAL SPINE

Focus on: Isolated movement (rotation) of the cervical spine. Do *not* rotate the shoulders and thoracic spine. This is a comparatively simple exercise. However, don't be tempted to skip it, because it acts as preparation for the later, more difficult drills for the vestibular system (see p. 127). Furthermore, this exercise can be used very successfully for test-retest situations: You'll find out in which direction you're better able to rotate. Improvement of your ability to rotate the more restricted side is a positive retest result.

2

How to do it:
— Try a test.
— Find the most prominent vertebra you can feel with your fingers. It's easiest to feel at the base of your neck. This vertebra is C7. Slide your fingers to the right of this vertebra and massage this point for 20 to 30 seconds.

3

4

5

1 *Find the large vertebra called C7 with your fingers.*

2 *Sensory before motor: Massage C7.*

3 *Starting position and end position.*

4 *Slowly rotate your head and breathe in.*

5 *Test in both directions.*

— Start in a Neutral Standing Position ("push your crown through the ceiling"—p. 70).

— Begin the movement with your eyes: First look to the left, and then rotate your head as far to the left as possible. You can imagine your chin is resting on a table, and you're rotating your chin to the left.

— Try to begin the movement from the point you massaged on the right next to C7. You can place your right middle finger on this point and begin to turn your head. Try to feel how the transverse process your right middle finger is currently resting on moves forward when you turn to the left. Remain in the end position for a short time.

— Breathe in for two seconds as you rotate, hold your breath for around two seconds in the end position, and then breathe out for four seconds as you rotate back to the center. Hold your breath for around two seconds in the central end position, which is also the starting position. Repeat the sequence five times. At this breathing rhythm, you will need 10 seconds per rotation (which corresponds to our "slow motion speed"), with an extended exhalation phase. By the way, this is a physiological respiratory frequency that's ideal for reducing pain (Jafari et al. 2017).

— Repeat the cervical spine rotation in the other direction—to the right— and retest.

YES-YES MOVEMENT

FLEXION AND EXTENSION OF THE CERVICAL SPINE

Focus on: Isolated movement of the cervical spine. Do not stretch and flex the thoracic vertebrae at the same time! This drill is also very good for using in a test-retest situation. How far can you extend your head and how far can you flex it?

How to do it:

— Try a test.
— Rub the cervical spine at the base of your skull with your fingertips for around 20 seconds. Stand in a neutral position. Look straight ahead. Then look up, and tilt the back of your head back and down and your face to the ceiling. Remain in the end position for a short time. Then look down, and pull your chin in the direction of your larynx so your cervical spine flexes forward. Now look up again, and start moving your head from this forward flexed position into the backward extended position. Keep your breathing relaxed and breathe slowly in and out through your nose. Do five repetitions in slow motion (around 10 seconds for each repetition).
— Retest, and record the result in the table.

The eyes "lead": First look up.

Then "pull" your head back.

Look down and flex your neck.

Flex your neck as far as possible.

LATERAL FLEXION OF THE CERVICAL SPINE

LATERAL FLEXION

Focus on: Initiate the movement from cervical vertebra C7.

1

How to do it:
— Try a test.
— Rub the area around the seventh cervical vertebra (C7) with your fingertips. It's the vertebra that stands out prominently at the base of your neck, and the transition to the thoracic spine—it's very easy to feel. The neutral standing position is the starting position. Actively pull your chin slightly down and back toward your Adam's apple so you can feel your cervical vertebrae bend slightly at the nape of your neck. Hold this position, and then tilt your head slightly to the side and away from the central axis, bringing your ear closer to your shoulder. Important: Try to move your neck from C7—that's why we sensorially pre-activated this area.
— Repeat the movement five times at our "slow motion" speed. You can also experiment with the rhythm of your breathing. Hold your breath for two seconds, breathe in for two seconds, hold your breath for two seconds, and then breathe out for four seconds. Most people find it more relaxing to combine the breathing-in phase with tilting the head sideways towards the shoulder. Try it yourself.
— Retest, record the result in the table, and test the other side.

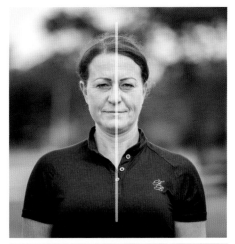

2

1 *Only tilt your head to the side.*
2 *The neutral standing position is the starting position.*
3 *Alex rotates her head slightly to the left, which shouldn't happen!*

3

79

Start in the neutral standing position. Then pull your chin back and down.

Push the clown nose forward as if on a rail.

Pull the clown nose as far back as possible.

THE HEN

GLIDE THE CERVICAL SPINE BACK AND FORTH

Focus on: When pulling back your chin, try to have slight flexion in the upper cervical spine when you glide back.

How to do it:
— Try a test.
— Rub the cervical spine at the base of your skull with your fingertips for around 20 seconds. In the starting position, actively pull your chin slightly down and back toward your Adam's apple so that you can feel your cervical vertebrae flex slightly at the nape of your neck. Now imagine you're wearing a red clown nose, and push the tip of your clown nose as far forward as possible (we call this *protraction*, by the way), breathing out through your nose as you do so. Then pull the nose back again, and pull your chin in the direction of your Adam's apple (this movement is called *retraction*), breathing in through your nose. Repeat this sequence—in "slow motion"—around five times. Stay relaxed as you do so. Limit the tension in your body to the absolute minimum necessary. Take the time to learn the movement and experiment with it.
— Retest, and record the result in the table.

THE PECKING HEN

GLIDE THE FLEXED CERVICAL SPINE BACK-AND-FORTH

Focal point: The aim is to achieve slight flexion in the upper cervical spine when pulling back your chin.

How to do it:
— Try a test.
— Rub the cervical spine from the base of your skull to C7 with your fingertips for around 20 seconds. Begin in the Neutral Standing Position. In the starting position, pull your chin slightly down and back toward your Adam's apple, such that you can feel your cervical vertebrae flex slightly at the nape of your neck.
— Now look down at your front along your chest, bending your head as far forward as you can without moving your thoracic spine.

— Now push your chin down toward your chest—and don't be surprised if you can only move an inch or so. That's completely normal. Finish up in the end position. Now for the more important part of the movement: Pull your chin as far up as possible while your head remains in the flexed position, up and back, such that your head makes a slightly forward rolling movement. The aim is to achieve maximum flexion of the upper cervical spine. Breathe through your nose, keeping your breathing relaxed; experiment to find out the best time for you to breathe in or out in order for you to relax as you are doing the movement.

— Retest, and record the result in the table.

1 *Sensory activation of cervical vertebra C7.*

2 *Lower your head, look down, and flex your neck.*

3 *Imagine your head making a rolling movement.*

4 *Important: Your neck must stay flexed.*

1

2

3

4

THE HEN IN A SIDEWAYS POSITION

GLIDE BACK AND FORTH IN A SIDEWAYS POSITION

Focus on: Create flexion in the upper cervical spine.

How to do it:

— Try a test.
— Rub your upper cervical spine with your fingertips for around 20 seconds. The Neutral Standing Position is the starting position.
— Pull your chin slightly down and back toward your Adam's apple, such that you can feel your cervical vertebrae flex slightly at the nape of your neck. Hold this position and tilt your head sideways to the right—keeping your head on this tilted axis—and now we're back at the clown nose again: Push the nose forward toward the opposite wall (protraction) as far as possible with your head in the same tilted position. Breathe out through your nose as you do so. Then pull the clown nose back in the direction of the wall behind you (retraction), breathing in through your nose as you do so. Keep your head in the sideways tilted position. It's completely normal to feel a stretching sensation in the left of the nape of your neck. Remain in the end position for two to three seconds, and then repeat the entire sequence five times in "slow motion." Your breathing should be in sync with the movement of your head: nose forward, breathe out; nose back, breathe in.
— It can often be helpful to use a mirror to see whether you're keeping your head in a tilted position or compensating with rotational movements. Use the image in the mirror to check. Repeat the movement five times in "slow motion."
— Retest, record the result in the table, and test the other side.

Head to the side, chin back.

Push your head forward.

Do the same on the other side.

Hold your head on a tilted axis.

AUTONOMIC NERVOUS SYSTEM

The Hen Drill—which focuses on retraction (pulling back)—comes very close to mobilization of the sagittal suture of the skull. Although this suture will be ossified in most people over 30, this drill can still gently mobilize the *dura mater* and the nerve endings in it. Experience has shown that this drill helps many people activate the muscles responsible for bending the upper body forward. Try a few sit-ups and sit-ups with rotation before and after as a test-retest. This drill is also good for mobilizing the cervical spine in the area around C1 and C2, and stabilizing the associated muscles. An important nerve runs directly in front of these two vertebrae—the *vagus nerve*. This is our largest cranial nerve and is responsible for supporting regeneration processes and controlling the immune, digestive, and cardiovascular systems, and many others. This exercise is a good opportunity to stimulate the vagus nerve, an important part of our autonomic nervous system.

BEND AND STRETCH THE THORACIC SPINE

Focus on: Bend and stretch the thoracic spine.

How to do it:
— Try a test.

— Firmly rub along your sternum from top to bottom with the knuckles of your fingers. If somebody can help you, you can get them to firmly rub the vertebrae on your back—around 4 inches (10 centimeters) above to 4 inches below the bottom edges of your shoulder blades.
— The Neutral Standing Position is the starting position.

Alex concentrates on feeling her thoracic spine as I rub and tap it.

Push the ball into my hand.

Pull the ball back.

— Use your fingers to touch the area between your pectoral muscles. You can also use a tennis ball to gently press against these areas. Now breathe in slowly and deeply through your nose, and push the tennis ball far forward at the same time, as if you wanted to push it through the opposite wall. Then move in the other direction, pulling the ball toward the wall behind you and breathing out as you do so. Try to get the ball as far back as possible. Make sure you stay relaxed; you don't need excessive muscle tension for this mobilization. Do 5 to 6 repetitions. You can do this movement standing or sitting. Always breathe in sync with the movement. Pay attention to your line of sight.

— Retest, record the result in the table, and test the other side.

I use finger pressure to mark two points on the thoracic spine: Bring these points closer together and push the ball forward, looking up and breathing in.

Now move the fingers as far apart as possible. Pull the ball to the wall behind you. Breathe out, look at your chest. Create maximum flexion!

Pull one shoulder down.

Flex your thoracic spine.

Stretch your thoracic spine.

Side view: flexed position.

BEND THE THORACIC SPINE IN A SIDEWAYS POSITION

Focus on: Flex your thoracic spine to the side and stretch it in a sideways position.

How to do it:

— Try a test.
— In principle, the sequence of this exercise is the same as the sequence of the exercise on page 83, but it starts in a different position, with the thoracic spine flexed to the side.
— Do 5 to 6 repetitions.
— Retest, record the result in the table, and test the other side.

Find the two "bumps"—the two iliac crests.

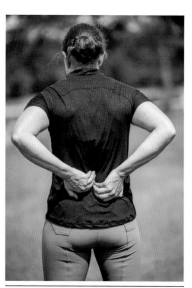

Place your fingers on your spine from the middle out.

"Can you feel where you should generate the movement from?"

LUMBAR SPINE IN A SEMICIRCLE FORWARD

Focus on: Put both hands on your lumbar spine, and find both iliac crests, around 2 inches (5 centimeters) to the left and right of the center of your back. Find the spine between them. From the center point out, place all the fingers of your left hand and your right hand, apart from your thumbs, together on your spine, and say "hello" to your lumbar spine. Vigorously rub the vertebrae. This is where you want to generate the movement from.

How to do it:
— Try a test.
— Begin in the Neutral Standing Position with your knees slightly bent. Your pelvis should remain upright the entire time. First, bend sideways to the left from the center, allowing both arms to hang down loosely, with your head tilted to the left. Now imagine you want to use your head to draw a semicircle from the left to the front, and then from the front to the right. Allow your right shoulder to fall forward, look at the floor, and begin to trace this semicircle very slowly with your head. Make sure you feel and move the focal area during the movement. You can bend a little farther forward if you need to. Complete the arc on the right side, pull your left shoulder out of the rotation, and then slowly straighten up again and come back to the center.
— Repeat the movement in the other direction. It's very important to move in "slow motion" at the start of the exercise—don't take any less than 30 seconds per semicircle.
— Retest, record the result in the table, and test the other side.

Alex should generate the movement in the lumbar spine.

I leave my fingers there so that Alex can keep checking.

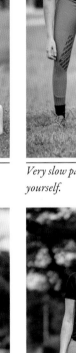

Very slow pace, so you can correct yourself.

You need to be careful and pay attention when doing the semicircle. Allow yourself lots of time.

30 seconds is a long time. You might even need 60 seconds. Keep making sure that you can feel your lumbar spine.

Finish the movement exactly where you started: in a neutral standing position looking straight ahead.

1

2

3

4

1 *Alex bends to the right...*

2 *... and then to the back; her head follows.*

3 *And from there, to the left...*

4 *... and then back to the starting position.*

pelvis should remain upright the entire time. First bend to the side from the center to the right, allowing both arms to hang down loosely, with your head tilted to the right. Now imagine you want to use your head to draw a semicircle from the right to the back, and then from the back to the left. Allow your left shoulder to fall back, and look at the ceiling; your cervical spine sinks down to the back. Begin to very slowly draw that semicircle with your head. Make sure you feel and move the focal area during this exercise. You can bend a little farther back if you need to. Complete the arc on the left side, and pull your right shoulder out of the rotation; slowly straighten up again, and come back to the center.

— Repeat the movement in the other direction. It's very important to move in "slow motion" at the start of the exercise— don't take any less than 30 seconds per semicircle.

— Retest, record the result in the table, and test the other side.

LUMBAR SPINE IN A SEMICIRCLE BACKWARD

Focus on: See exercise on page 86.

How to do it:
— Try a test.
— Begin in the Neutral Standing Position with your knees slightly bent. Your

BALANCE BOOST

Lumbar spine circles, especially when done faster (once you've gotten the hang of them), have the potential to temporarily influence the balance organs in the inner ear, as well as the somatic components of the vestibular system, probably in the kidneys; therefore, this exercise can change your perception of your balance.

STRAIGHTEN AND TILT PELVIS

Focus on: Tilting forward and straightening, or rather tilting the iliac crests back.

How to do it:

— Try a test.

— Rub your right and left iliac crests. Your feet should be shoulder-width apart and your knees should be slightly bent and should stay that way. Place your fingers on your left and right iliac crests. Imagine your pelvis as a paper fan. How do you move a fan? You start the movement from the handle, and move the top of the fan back and forth slightly. However, you should "fan" with your pelvis slowly and carefully; you don't want to make a draft.

— Here's another image to help you get a feel for when your pelvis is straight: Imagine you, like our prehistoric ancestors, have a tail instead of a sacrum. This tail reaches down to the ground and is very stable. You now want to firmly push the tail into the floor behind you; this straightens up your pelvis. Slightly lift the tail, and your pelvis tilts forward; push the tail into the floor again, and your pelvis returns to a straightened position.

— Practice for a minute, making sure the musculature of your lumbar spine is as relaxed as possible and your abdominal muscles are also relaxed.

— Retest, and record the result in the table.

FOCAL POINT: PELVIS POSITION
This exercise might have changed your understanding of what an upright pelvis feels like. Using your new skill, pay attention to the position of your pelvis when you're standing in a neutral position.

The knees should stay slightly bent.

Straighten your pelvis—"push your tail into the floor."

Tilt your pelvis—"lift your tail."

Upright pelvis.

Pelvis tilted to the left.

Pelvis tilted forward.

Pelvis tilted to the right.

PELVIC ROTATIONS

Focus on: Only move your pelvis, and don't speed up or slow down. You're only allowed to move your pelvis—not your upper body, not the rest of your spine, not your shoulders, and not your head. Everything else stays still; only your pelvis circles.

How to do it:

— Try a test.
— Imagine there's a round tray with a small marble on it lying on your pelvis. This tray is raised at the sides. Move your pelvis so the marble rolls in a circle around the edges of the tray at an even speed. Allow the marble to do around 10 circles, then change direction.
— Retest, and record the result in the table.

1

1 Palm facing down.
2 Flex the wrist.
3 Thumb points up to the center.

2

3

4

5

FIGURE EIGHTS WITH THE HANDS

Focus on: Maximum movement in the wrist in all directions, with the fingers staying stretched out. Make sure you keep your elbows and shoulders still and don't move them.

How to do it:

— Try a test.
— Vigorously rub your right wrist.
— Start in Neutral Standing Position. Raise your right forearm into a horizontal position, with your palm facing down. Stretch your fingers and push your palm right down until your fingertips are pointing to the floor. From this position, pull your thumb up until it's pointing to the right—your wrist will rotate outward as you do this, and still has maximum bend.
— Now push the back of your hand down until your wrist is extended to the maximum. Move your thumb up again, with your wrist rotating at the same time, until your thumb is pointing left and your palm is facing forward. Now push your wrist down again until your fingertips are pointing down. Practice drawing this sideways figure eight in the air.
— Retest, record the result in the table, and then repeat with your left hand and retest again.

6

7

8

4 Stretch your wrist from here.
5 Your palm faces up.
6 Your palm faces forward.
7 Thumbs point up to the center.
8 Back to the starting position.

FORWARD SHOULDER CIRCLES

Focus on: The shoulder joint. Visualize movement in the joint.

How to do it:
— Try a test.
— Start in Neutral Standing Position. Begin with your right shoulder.
— Extend your right arm, and raise it into a horizontal position in front of your body, with your fist lightly closed. From your shoulder, move your extended arm in a circle of approximately 3 feet (1 meter) in diameter. Your elbow should always be completely straight. The speed should be "slow" to "slow motion."
— Make sure your spine doesn't rotate. The axes of your body should remain completely stable. Only your shoulder joint should move.
— Retest, record the result in the table, and then repeat on the left side and retest again.

Cross-body: small circles on the other side of the centerline.

CROSS-BODY SHOULDER CIRCLES

Focus on: During the movement, focus on the shoulder joint and therefore the area of the circle that requires a lot of muscular tension in the pectoral muscles.

How to do it:
— Try a test.
— Start in Neutral Standing Position. Begin with the right shoulder.

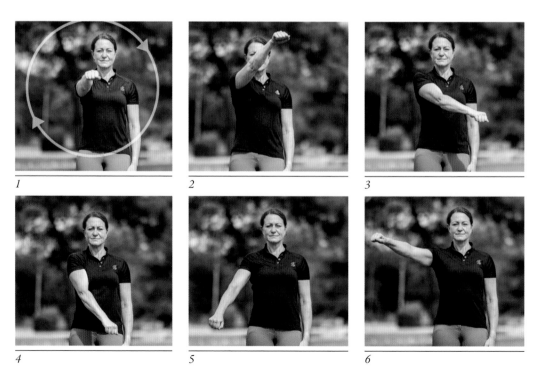

1

2

3

4

5

6

— Extend your right arm, and raise it into a horizontal position in front of your body, with your fist lightly closed. Move your shoulder so your right fist is in front of your left shoulder, keeping your arm fully extended. You should now feel your right pectoral muscles tense. Very good! Do small circles in this position. Your elbows should always be completely straight. Choose a "slow" to "slow motion" speed.

— Make sure your spine doesn't rotate. Keep your head and eyes aimed straight ahead. The axes of your body should remain completely stable. Only your shoulder joint should move.

— Retest, record the results in the table, and then repeat on the right side and retest again.

SIDE SHOULDER CIRCLES

Focus on: Movement in the shoulder joint.

How to do it:
— Try a test.
— Start in Neutral Standing Position. Begin with your right shoulder.
— Extend your right arm, and raise it into a horizontal position next to your body, with your fist lightly closed. Move your shoulder so your extended arm points horizontally to the right. From this position, make big circles at the side of your body. Your eyes should look to the right, but your head should be straight. Your elbows should always be completely straight. The speed should be "slow" to "slow motion."

— Make sure your spine and head don't rotate. The axes of your body should remain completely stable. Only your shoulder joint should move.

— Retest, record your results in the table, and then repeat on the left side and retest again.

— Try it at a different speed.

Raise your arm out to the side until it is in a horizontal position.

Only your shoulder should move, nothing else.

The circle should always be the same size.

Draw a circle—no corners or edges.

Hip joint in "neutral."   *Rehab position, inward rotation.*   *Rehab position, outward rotation.*

HIP CIRCLES IN FOUR POSITIONS

Focus on: Movement in the hips; finding the Rehab Position.

How to do it:

— Find the Rehab Position—which is to say, first we need to work out which position is the "Rehab Position" for you. Start in Neutral Standing Position. Support yourself against a wall or the back of a chair with one hand to keep your balance. Stand on your left leg and raise your right leg in front of you slightly, from the hip, keeping it straight, so your heel is around 8 inches (20 centimeters) above the ground. Now rotate your thigh bone inward toward the center of your body, without rotating your pelvis at the same time. Feel how easy or difficult it is for you to hold this position for a few seconds. Relax.

— Start again, but this time, rotate your thigh bone outward at the hip. Compare the level of difficulty required to maintain this position. The position you find more difficult to hold is your "Rehab Position." Test your Rehab Position for both hip joints. Mark the table below to keep track.

FORWARD HIP CIRCLES

Focus on: Hip joints.

How to do it:

— Try a test (if you have discrepancies in the movement of your shoulder joint, then do the Shoulder Tests from page 92).

— Start in Neutral Standing Position. Support yourself on the back of a chair with one hand. Stand on your left leg and raise your right leg in front of you from the hip; then move your hip into the Rehab Position. Move your thigh bone from the hip joint, such that your heel describes the biggest circle possible.

Rehab Position in the Hip	Right	Left
Inward rotation		
Outward rotation		
Both rotations equally		

Make a circle ... | *... in front of your body.* | *Nice and big and round!*

— Make sure you keep your hip joint in the rehab position for the entire circular movement! And remember: A circle is round! The speed should be "slow" to "slow motion."
— Make sure your pelvis doesn't rotate or tilt to the side. Maintain a neutral, one-legged stance with your spine long. Only your hip should move, not your ankle! Keep your ankle loose and relaxed.
— Start with two clean circles in a clockwise direction, and then do two circles in a counterclockwise direction.
— Retest, record the result in the table, and then repeat on the other side and retest again.

CROSS-BODY HIP CIRCLES

Focus on: Hip joints.

How to do it:
— Try a test (if you have discrepancies in the movement of your shoulder joints, then you should definitely do the Shoulder Tests from page 92).
— Start in Neutral Standing Position. Support yourself on the back of a chair with one hand. Stand on your left leg and raise your right leg in front of you from the hip. Move your hips into the rehab position, then pull your leg to the left and cross it over the centerline of your body. Move your thigh bone from the hip joint, such that your heel describes the biggest circle possible on the left side in front of you. Make sure you keep your hip joint in the rehab position through-out the entire circular movement.

Cross-body: Draw a circle on the other side of the centerline.

— You're aiming for the biggest possible round circle, at a "slow motion" speed. No pelvic rotation.
— Two circles in each direction.
— Retest, record the result in the table, and then repeat on the other side and retest again.

SIDEWAYS HIP CIRCLES

Focus on: Hip joints.

How to do it:
— Try a test (I'd suggest the Shoulder Test on page 92 or Balance Tests from page 127).
— Start in Neutral Standing Position. Support yourself on the back of a chair with one hand. Stand on your left leg and raise your right leg in front of you from the hip. Take up the Rehab Position. Move your leg next to your body, and make a circle next to your body. Keep your hip in the Rehab Position. You're aiming for the biggest possible round circle, at a "slow motion" speed. Two circles in each direction.

— Retest, record the result in the table, and then repeat on the other side and retest again.

BACKWARD HIP CIRCLES

Focus on: Hip; keep your pelvis upright when stretching your hip.

How to do it:
— Try a test (I'd suggest the Shoulder Test on page 92 or Balance Test on page 127).
— Start in Neutral Standing Position. Straighten your pelvis. Support yourself on the back of a chair with one hand. Stand on your left leg and raise your right leg in front of you from the hip. Take up the Rehab Position. Move your leg as far behind your body as possible—without tilting your pelvis. Make a circle

---

SMALLEST CIRCLE

This circle is the smallest possible circle. It simply isn't possible to extend the hip all that far, for most people, so don't be surprised.

Side: next to your body.

Back: behind your body.

Start with your leg stretched out to the front.

Push your knee in.

Move it forward.

Outward.

Through a circle.

And back to extension.

behind your body, to the right. You're aiming for the biggest possible round circle, at a "slow motion" speed. Two circles in each direction.

— Retest, record the result in the table, and then repeat on the other side and retest again.

KNEE CIRCLES

Focus on: Generate lots of movement in the knee joint.

How to do it:
— Try a test.
— Start in Neutral Standing Position. You're aiming for your right knee. Rub it vigorously with both hands until it feels slightly warmer. Take a normal-size step

forward with your right leg. Support yourself with one hand somewhere, without changing your posture. The aim of the exercise is to move your front knee in a horizontal circle. Start with your knee joint completely straight. Imagine you wanted to swing a hula hoop around your knee—in slow motion.

— From the extended position, move your knee first in, then forward, then out,

MOVEMENT IN THE KNEE JOINT

Your ankle and your hip joint obviously also move in this exercise. However, your attention should be focused on the movement of your knee joint. It's important for your knee joint to "lock into" the stretched position after every complete circle.

then backward, back to the starting position. The sole of your front foot stays on the floor, and your center of gravity and your spine move forward.

— You can lift the heel of your back foot off the ground. Try to make the biggest, deepest circle possible. Take note of where corners and edges try to appear in what should be a circular movement. If necessary, reduce your speed and try to eliminate these corners. Make sure your upper body remains stable and upright, and your pelvis doesn't rotate but always stays pointing straight forward.

— Retest, record the results in the table, and then repeat on the other side and retest again.

TILT ANKLE OUTWARD

Focus on: The lower ankle joint is below your left outer ankle where you rubbed it.

How to do it:
— Try a test.
— Rub the area about 1 inch (2 to 3 centimeters) below your outside left ankle *(malleolus lateralis)*. This is where you want to generate movement from. Start in Neutral Standing Position. Take a small step forward with your left foot so your left heel is approximately one foot's width from the tip of your right toes. Now imagine your left heel is a small boat rocking on the water. The boat lists and is pushed left, tipping to the outside until water flows in over the gunwale. Try to control this movement in your ankle only, not from your hip. Push the boat slowly but firmly to the side; allow it to fill up with water for two to three seconds, and then slowly return to the starting position, with no corners or edges in the movement. Repeat this sequence around five times.
— Retest, record the results in the table,

Generate the movement from here.

Keep your spine long.

Push the boat to the side.

and then repeat on the other side and retest again.

— Rotate your foot inward a little and repeat the drill in this new position approximately five times.

— Now rotate your foot outward a little and repeat the drill in this new position approximately five times.

PULL TOES STRAIGHT

Focus on: Find the underside of the ankle bones on each side of your foot, and then move your fingers along them until your fingers meet at the front of your foot, where you will find a bony cleft that runs across your forefoot. We want to achieve movement and opening of the cleft at this point.

How to do it:
— Try a test.
— Rub the focal point until you can feel it well. Start in Neutral Standing Position. Balance yourself against a wall using your left hand. Move your right leg back and put your bent toes on the floor with your toenails down. Your right hip should be slightly extended, and your right thigh should be at least slightly behind your left thigh.
— You can intensify and reduce the stretch by slightly flexing or extending your supporting leg. Bend, hold for two to three seconds, and then come back up again. Do approximately three to five repetitions.
— Retest, record the result in the table, and then repeat on the other side and retest again.

1

1 Rub the focal point.
2 Put your toes on the ground.
3 Pull your toes forward, without slipping.

2

3

Push the focal point out, along with your thigh. *Try to "open" the focal point.*

PULL TOES OUT

Focus on: Find the bottom edge of your outside ankle and trace your fingertip along it toward your forefoot, with slight pressure. After about an inch (2 to 3 centimeters), you will feel a small, soft hole. That's where to focus.

How to do it:
— Try a test.
— Rub the focal point until you can feel it well. Start in Neutral Standing Position. Balance yourself against a wall using either your left or right hand. Take your right leg back and place your bent toes on the floor, with your toenails pointing forward. Your right hip should be slightly extended, and your right thigh should be slightly behind the thigh of your supporting left leg. Now push the focal point out as if you wanted to push it into the ground. To

feel a stretch in the focal point, you might need to push your thigh slightly out from the hip. You can intensify and reduce the stretch by slightly flexing or extending your supporting leg. Bend, hold for two to three seconds, and then come back up again.
— Do approximately three to five repetitions.
— Retest, record the results in the table, and then repeat on the other side and retest again.

ISOMETRIC FULL BODY CONTRACTION

Focus on: Hold and then explosively relax a high level of tension in all your muscles. You'll find you tend to hold your breath during this exercise. However, that isn't necessary. You can tense your muscles, hold the tension, and keep breathing.

Efficient movement isn't just about being able to tense your muscles; it's also about being able to relax them.

How to do it:
— Try a test.
— Start in Neutral Standing Position. Tense the following areas of the body one after the other. Hold the tension in all areas until you finish. Give yourself two to three seconds between each step.
— Tense your feet. Okay, now your lower legs. Then your upper legs. Buttocks, stomach, back, shoulders—check whether you're still holding the tension in all previous areas as you go—and continue with your arms and fists, clenching them tightly! The muscles of your face, too. Tense everything; hold, hold, hold, approximately three to five seconds, and then breathe out explosively, like a burst balloon, and release all at once. Loosely shake out your arms and legs.
— Repeat this sequence three to five times.
— Retest and record the result in the table.

1   2   3   4

1 First, tense your legs, ...
2 ... then your buttocks, stomach, back, arms, ...
3 ... hands, and face. Hold everything and ...
4 ... explosive relaxation!

NEURO-RIDER VISION
— *See Better*

TRAINING YOUR VISUAL SYSTEM

Congratulations! You've already achieved so much! Now let's continue with drills for the visual system. It took me years to understand the visual system in a way that enabled me to work with it. It's complicated—but these Vision Drills are very effective.

Saccade: Visual perception of information is the basis for acting quickly.

BETTER VISION FOR POSTURE AND STABILITY

Most of us weren't taught much about how the eyes and vision work, and we definitely weren't taught to train our eyes and visual system in the brain just like we can train our heart and muscles, or skills such as strength and flexibility. You can exert a powerful influence on your brain with these basic exercises—and eye exercises aren't just beneficial for riders, they're genuine anti-aging medicine for everyone.

Remember, your brain needs enough fuel (glucose and oxygen) to function and build changes into itself permanently, in addition to the activation you'll achieve with these exercises.

WITH OR WITHOUT GLASSES?

— If possible, do all the drills without glasses, unless you are no longer able to identify your visual targets at a distance of 2 to 3 feet (0.5 to 1 meter). If you can't tell the difference between your thumb and your index finger at that distance, then put on your glasses.

— If you wear glasses with a very high or very low diopter value and very small frames, they can act like a "cage" for your eyes.

— Small glasses and glasses with thick frames create a subconscious limit for the movement of the eyes, and therefore the eye muscles, and reduce the neuronal activation of the cranial nerves involved. If your eye muscles don't pull strongly on your eyeball from all sides, or don't have a healthy muscle tone, then your eyeball and cornea will become more and more crooked. This is called *astigmatism*. The solution is to wear glasses with larger lenses and thin or no frames.

— If you've lost an eye or if you can only see very little through one or both eyes, then visual training is very important. The muscles of your eyes are still there—and they still need to move. The same goes for the nerves that move the muscles; they'll be glad to finally be able to "fire" again.

I WEAR VARIFOCAL (PROGRESSIVE) LENSES. THEY'RE GREAT, AREN'T THEY?

Well…8 out of 10 clients who come to me wearing varifocal lenses are dealing with massive cervical and thoracic spine problems. It hardly occurs to anybody that there could be a link. However, the causal link is obvious, and there are neurological reasons for it, too. Varifocal lenses take away the job of the small muscles that change the shape of your lenses so that objects at different distances can be correctly displayed on your retina. If you wear varifocals, you raise your head to be able to see close up, instead of sharpening the lens in your eye, and vice versa. This is unnatural. The muscles (*ciliary muscles*) that shape your lenses are activated by a cranial nerve in the midbrain—the *nervus oculomotorius*. Put very simply, the

HOW DOES IT WORK?

The procedure for the Vision Drills is the same as for the exercises for proprioception (see p. 65). Read the descriptions, and do your tests; then do the drills as described, and do your retests.

midbrain is an area that ensures, among other things, correct modulation of the muscular tension of the flexor muscles throughout the whole of the body, including the neck.

As a result, the midbrain is less active in people who wear varifocal lenses because the *nervus oculomotorius* is only working part time—which has a negative effect on muscle tension. Wearing varifocal lenses results in poorer stamina of the deep neck flexors; the head tilts forward, and the cervical vertebrae are permanently overextended and no longer in balance. People who wear varifocal lenses are very likely to pay a high price for their convenience. The solution is wearing two pairs of glasses—and training.

THE DOSE MAKES THE MEDICINE

Remember: The dose makes the medicine. Start with the recommendations given. If a drill doesn't work, then repeat it at a higher dose, a different speed, or, if necessary, a lower dose, and retest to see which helps most.

PS: This also applies to all your "Neutral" drills from the section on proprioception. Many people will need more repetitions and more speed than I have suggested as a starting point.

Tests and Drills Visual System—Vision	On page	Both Eyes			Left			Right		
		Neutral	Rehab	Power	Neutral	Rehab	Power	Neutral	Rehab	Power
Gaze Stabilization at Nine Points	107									
Left up										
Left horizontal										
Left down										
Center up										
Center										
Center down										
Right up										
Right horizontal										
Right down										
Gentle Gaze Tracking	108									
To the right										
To the left										
Up										
Down										
To the top left										
To the bottom left										
To the top right										
To the bottom right										
Saccades	110									
To the right										
To the left										
Optokinetics	112									
Movement direction to right										
Movement direction to left										
Cross-o-Matic/Pencil Press-Up	114									
Eye Circles	117									
Peripheral Vision	118									
Near-Far Jumps	120									
Pinhole Glasses	122									
Colored Glasses	123									
Binasal/Uninasal Occlusion	124									
Earplugs	125									

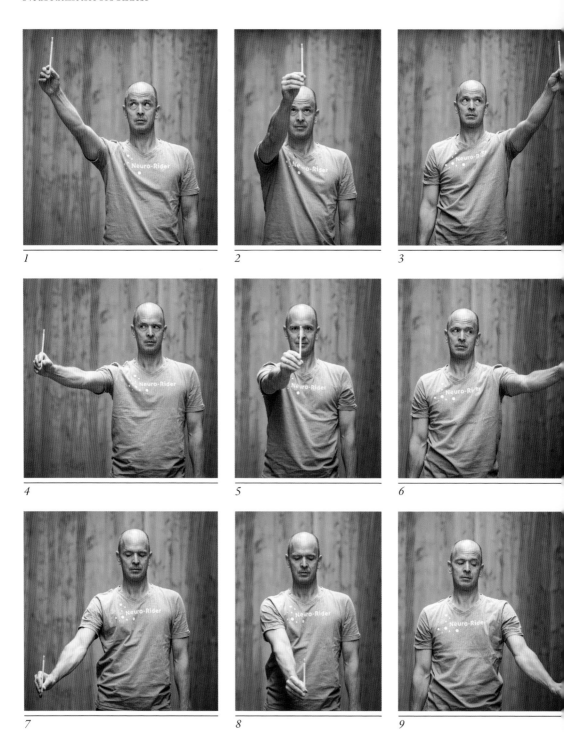

1 – 9   *Gaze Stabilization at Nine Points: Although this drill might seem simple, it can be astonishingly effective. People should be able to look in any direction without their retest results getting worse. Can you find directions that influence your performance?*

GAZE STABILIZATION AT NINE POINTS

Focus on: Can I see a target clearly when I look at it? Gaze stabilization is a very important, fundamental skill that has a major influence on our head and neck stability and helps with precision of movement in our entire spine. This exercise seems very easy, but neurologically it's very complex. Gaze stabilization is isometric training for our eye muscles. It trains our central cerebellum and our ability to ignore distracting stimuli—it's a skill that can benefit anybody, and any athlete.

How to do it:
— Try a test.
— Begin in Neutral Standing Position. Start a timer: You're aiming for 30 seconds.
— Look at a central visual target at arm's length and at eye level for 30 seconds. Retest immediately afterward, and record the results in the table.
— Then change to the other eight positions, testing and retesting after each individual position, and record the results in the table.
— Make sure you only move your eyes and not your head.
— You must also make sure you can always see your target with both eyes.
— The challenge is to be able to keep your visual focus in one place for 30 seconds, without your eyes quivering, running, or becoming dry. Occasional blinking is normal.
— Adapt the duration of each individual position to your skills. If you need to start with five seconds, because you can feel your eyes quivering after five seconds, then that's okay. Build it up slowly until you can easily manage 30 seconds. Retest and record the result in the table.

INTENSIFICATION FOR MOVEMENT DRILLS

If you find an eye position that improves your retest results, then try making use of it while you're doing the movement drills from the previous chapters. Combine your Power Eye Position and a movement drill.

TRAINING TIPS: GAZE STABILIZATION

— Try a Rehab Movement Drill with a Power Eye Position, and check your retest. A useful eye position might help your brain and allow you to convert a Rehab Movement Drill into a Neutral Drill that doesn't provoke a threat reaction in your nervous system.
— But it can also work the other way around: Have you found an eye position that makes your retests worse? Use a Power Movement Drill, and do it for 20 to 30 seconds. Take a break of around 10 seconds, and then repeat the movement drill coupled with the Rehab Eye Position.
— Eye movements help back movements! Eye movements—especially gaze stabilization—activate the central cerebellum, and the central cerebellum is also responsible for precision in movements of the spine. By training eye movements, you're also helping your back become more stable and more able to move with precision.
— You can also do this drill with one eye. To do so, cover one eye with your hand or an eye patch. By testing and retesting, you can find out whether doing the drill with one eye is more effective for you.

— Think about fuel: Training eye movements is new and can be very strenuous. If you notice yourself becoming tired (your retests keep getting worse, or your eyes start running or become dry), then drink a glass of orange juice from time to time. Close your eyes, rub your hands to warm them up, and place them over your eyes. Gently massage the bony edges of your eye sockets, and blink a little. Do any of the breathing exercises from this book. All these things help relieve strain on the structures involved and increase the flow of oxygen and glucose to the brain.

GENTLE GAZE TRACKING IN EIGHT DIRECTIONS

Focus on: Can I see the target clearly when it's moving? "Gaze tracking" describes a gentle movement of the eyes, with the aim of watching a moving target and seeing it clearly. We can only move our eyes gently, without jumping, if we follow a visual target. Gentle gaze tracking isn't possible without a visual target.

First make sure you can see the target with both eyes in every direction. If you want to do gentle gaze tracking to the right, then you have to tightly shut your right eye when the target is in the furthest right end position, in order to be able to tell whether your left eye can see the target past your nose. When you've done that, then you know your freedom of movement in that direction.

How to do it:
— Try a test.
— Start in Neutral Standing Position. Fix your target in front of you at eye level. Move the target into the horizontal left position. You should take one second of time for the movement (if you say the word "Mississippi" out loud, then that's approximately one second). Make sure you can always see the target clearly and aren't moving your head. You can touch your chin with one hand to make sure your head isn't moving. Close your eyes in the end position. Bring the target back to the center, focus on it again, and repeat the tracking.
— Do around 10 to 20 repetitions.
— Retest and record the result in the table.
— Do the same with all other gaze tracking directions.

TRAINING TIPS: GAZE TRACKING
— You might find that you retest especially well after Gaze Tracking in one particular direction. Do more of that direction. Do it for as long as you like. Do it for as long as the retests are positive.

Can you see the target clearly? Gaze Tracking to the left.

Gaze Tracking to the right.

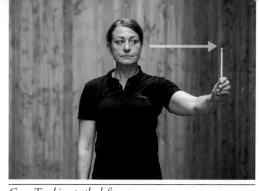

Gaze Tracking to the left.

Gaze Tracking up.

Gaze Tracking down.

Gaze Tracking from bottom right to top left.

Gaze Tracking from top right to bottom left.

Gaze Tracking from bottom left to top right.

Gaze Tracking from top left to bottom right.

— You might also notice that you lose your focus or sharpness in some areas of the tracking or that your eyes twitch or jump. This shouldn't happen. Practice eye circles in these areas, as described on page 117, but much smaller, perhaps only with a diameter of one hand's width.

— If you're having serious problems, you can do head movements before Gaze Stabilization. The signals from the canals in your vestibular system should support the movements of the eye muscles. For example, if you're experiencing problems with Gaze Tracking to the left, you should do a head movement to the right while focusing on your target. Do you notice that your eyes have to move gently to the left as you do so?

— Even if your retests are neutral, I recommend practicing gentle Gaze Tracking, because this stimulus is very good at activating your balance system.

— You can also do this with one eye, by covering the other eye with your hand or an eye patch. Through the test-retest strategy, you can find out whether doing this drill with one eye is more effective for you.

SACCADES

Focus on: Your head doesn't move, but your eyes do—can you see your target clearly? *Saccades* are very rapid eye movements from one focal point to another focal point. With Saccades, we should very quickly and very precisely find and see a visual target clearly, which allows us to rapidly understand what we're seeing.

How to do it:
— Try a test.
— Begin in a neutral position, and hold two visual focal points (business cards with letters or pencils work) at eye level, 18 inches (0.5 meters) in front of you.

1

2

3

1 *Starting position: Your head doesn't move.*

2 *Saccade to the right, and from there...*

3 *...Saccade to the left.*

Without moving your head, allow your eyes to jump back and forth from one target to the other. Allow your gaze to rest on the target until you can see it clearly and identify it. Start by doing Saccades for 30 seconds to a minute.
— Retest, and record the results in the table.
— Do the same with all other Saccade directions—vertical (from the top down), and along both diagonal axes.

TRAINING TIPS: SACCADES
— Improve the precision of your Saccades. There tend to be inaccuracies when doing Saccades. Either the eyes jump a little too far and then have to correct themselves by taking a small jump back (the technical term for this is *hypermetric*), or the eyes don't manage to jump all the way to the target and have to do another "mini-hop" to reach it (we call this *hypometric*). Without a coach watching your eyes, these issues can be difficult for you to identify. Just give the following a try and decide whether your eye movement feels better and more precise. You'll have to practice a little before it works.
— For hypometric Saccades: Do "micro-saccades, "lots of little jumps in one direction—for example, a series of sticky notes along a wall.
— After every Saccade, do six to seven small head movements, as if you are shaking your head "no," while your eyes remain on the target. Always press your fingers into the ball of the hand corresponding to the direction in which you are doing the saccade. This might seem strange at first, but you've no doubt heard of the concept of hand-eye coordination. This uses the same areas of the cerebellum that are strongly involved in "coordination control" between the ocular-motor and manual-motor system.

— For hypermetric Saccades: Do "micro-head-eye Saccades," moving your head and eyes from target to target at the same time. Make sure the distance to the target is very small (micro!). After every Saccade, do Gaze Tracking in the opposite direction.
— Test and retest, and record the results.
— You can also do this drill with your weaker eye. Through the test-retest strategy, you can find out whether doing the drill with one eye is more effective for you.
— Use 5 to 10 sticky notes for a series of Saccades in one direction.

IMPORTANT!
Every Saccade direction has a different profile for its brain activation pattern. For example, Saccades to the left activate the right frontal lobes, along with the pons in the left brainstem and the left cerebellum. If you have a stability problem with one side of your body, an isolated series of Saccades in just one direction can be a very helpful stimulus. Equally, if you have a problem with accuracy of movement on one side of your body, then the cerebellum is responsible for this.

Test whether 30 to 50 saccades (in one direction only) have an influence on your results in the Hand RAPS cerebellum test (see p. 59).

OPTOKINETICS

Focus on: This drill activates what is known as *optokinetic nystagmus*. This reflective eye movement stabilizes the eyes while you're following a large visual scene. This happens when you're traveling by train and you look out of the window and daydream: Your eyes remain "stuck" on part of the view out the window, follow it for a brief moment as the train goes past it (Gaze Tracking), and then jump to the next view (Saccade in the opposite direction). It's a very important reflex that only occurs in nature when we need to move or turn very quickly. It's no problem for young people, but it tends to be difficult for older people. However, it's trainable! Enter the following terms into a search engine: "optokinetic app" or "OptoDrum." You'll find an app that's compatible with all common operating systems. Choose an average stripe size and an average speed to start. Small screens do work, but the bigger the screen, the better.

— Try a test. Rotations and Hand RAPS are very good here.
— Set the app or hold your device so the stripes move from left to right. Start in Neutral Standing Position. Hold your device approximately one hand's length directly in front of your eyes. Relax and take a deep breath out and back in through your nose, and look at the screen passively. "Passively" means you don't have to do anything other than relax. After a short time, you should notice your eyes starting to make short tracking movements to the right, followed by Saccades to the left. That's good. Let it happen without trying to influence it. Begin with 30 seconds (and go up to a minute).
— Retest, and record the results in the table.
— Repeat the exercise with the stripes running from right to left.

TRAINING TIPS: REFLEXIVE EYE MOVEMENTS

— You can test the directions from the top down and from the bottom up separately. I haven't listed these in the table, but they can be very useful.
— If your eyes don't move and remain fixed, try a breathing exercise and then repeat this exercise.
— If you still don't experience any eye movements, do the exercise actively: Select one of the stripes that appears, track it with your gaze until it disappears, and then do a Saccade to find a new stripe; follow this one until it disappears, too, and so on.

1 *OptoDrum optokinetic reflex stimulation.*
2 *A smartphone is okay, but a tablet with its bigger screen is better.*

1

— Practice actively like this for one or two weeks, but keep trying to see whether the passive movement happens.
— For "neuro nerds": Gaze Tracking to the right activates the right *parietal lobes*, and Saccades to the left activate the right *frontal lobes*—and vice versa. A combination of these two eye movements (Saccades in one direction, followed by Gaze Tracking in the other direction) is therefore a useful combination for powerful activation of each hemisphere.
— Were your retests better, but you'd like even more activation for your right (left) hemisphere?
— Smell three different odors with your right nostril and identify the odors. This activates the right half of your brain.
— Do Movement Drills for the left side of your body—for example, figure eights with your hand (this activates your right motor cortex and your left cerebellum).
— Use your left palm to quickly and rhythmically slap the side of your left thigh (this activates the right motor cortex and your left cerebellum).
— Shine a powerful light source into your eyes from the left.
— You can also do this drill with your weaker eye. Through the test-retest strategy, you can find out whether doing the drill with one eye is more effective for you.

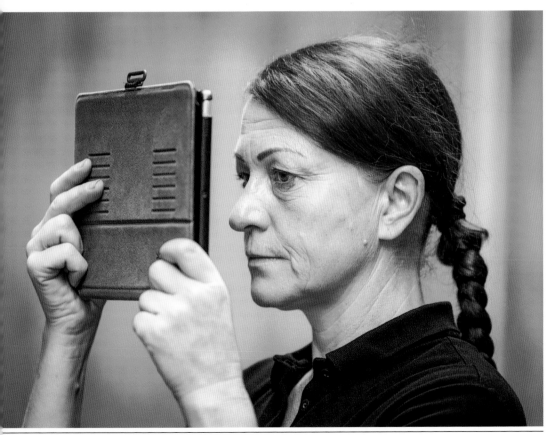

2

CROSS-O-MATIC OR PENCIL PRESS-UP

Focus on: Can you see your target without seeing double? The "Cross-o-Matic" trains the convergence and divergence movements of the eyes. *Convergence* describes a bilateral inward eye movement for looking at things close-up. *Divergence* describes the outward movement of the eyes for observing things that are moving away from us. During these movements, the eyes should work together as a team. Convergence and divergence movements are often impaired after minor concussions (Szymanowicz et al. 2012)—and almost all riders have experienced a minor concussion at least once.

How to do it:
You will need a pen, pencil or a business card, but you can also just use your thumbs. However, as with all the other exercises, it can be useful to have a letter or symbol on the target because our eyes "attach" better to shapes.
— Try a test.
— Start in Neutral Standing Position. Hold the visual target in front of you at eye level, at approximately arm's length, and focus on a point on this target. Pull your chin slightly down and back toward your Adam's apple, so your head tips slightly forward.
— Move the pen at eye level in a straight line centrally toward your eyes—precisely in the direction of the bridge of your nose, right between your eyes. It should take around three seconds to reach your nose. Count "one Mississippi, two Mississippi, three Mississippi."
— You should keep looking at the same point on the target the entire time. Slowly move the pen as close to your eyes as possible. Notice when the writing becomes blurred (no problem) or you see the target doubled.

From one arm's length distance ...

... pull the target toward you.

If you get positive results in a retest after the Cross-o-Matic, then do more of it. Would you like to know exactly what "more" means? For example, two sets of five repetitions, or one set of ten repetitions. If a drill works for you, it's a good idea to repeat short sets several times a day. Perhaps five times. If you can manage more, then you can safely do more. A set of six repetitions takes one minute. You could do five repeats of two sets, and then you'd have trained for ten minutes. That would be a great start. Try to synchronize the rhythm of your breathing with the eye movements—breathe slowly, and hold your breath at the points where you change direction.

If you see double, hold the pen shortly before the point where the double vision begins. The background of your field of vision will appear doubled. This is normal. However, the target should be clear. Hold the close position for two seconds.

— Stretch your arm out again, and move the target slowly away from your eyes and back to the starting position, taking three seconds in this direction, too. Stop for a moment here. And then do the whole thing again from the beginning. Start with three to five repetitions; one repetition should take around ten seconds.

— Retest, and record the results in the table.

ONE-EYED CROSS-O-MATIC

Focus on: Keep constant eye contact on the target with your weaker eye! It might be normal for this drill not to have any beneficial effect on you, but it could also be because you—like many other people—have a convergence weakness (*convergence insufficiency*) or are developing one. This bilateral vision disorder often occurs after concussions (Pearce et al. 2015). It is characterized by the eyes having a reduced ability to turn toward each other. People who are affected normally don't notice. Get a friend or partner to film your eye movements when you do the Cross-o-Matic, and see whether one eye is worse at moving into the convergence position, or is unable to hold it for as long as the other eye. Then see whether your "good" eye continues to focus on the focal point, while your "weak" eye drifts back to the central position. This minor defect can have significant motor consequences in the long term because parts of the midbrain and the pathways and cranial nerves that come from it are activated less—with effects on shoulder movements, and on the overall stability of the neck and upper body. You should therefore test and retest one-eyed triangular tracking with your weak eye. Cover your stronger eye with your hand or an eye patch.

— Try a test.

— Slowly move the visual target straight toward your eye. Stop. Slowly cross the centerline as far as possible without losing eye contact with the target. Stop. Slowly move back to the center, until the target has returned to the starting position. Stop at each key point for three seconds. To begin with, do three to five slow repetitions—although you're welcome to see how many you can tolerate. Finish the triangle tracking with a bilateral Cross-o-Matic to show your eyes they should work together as a team.

— Retest, and record the results in the table.

— You should also test your other eye if you aren't sure.

Close your "good" eye.

Stretch out your arm and move the target toward your eye.

Stop in the close area for a short time.

Pull the target across and track it.

Back to the starting point—repeat.

IMPORTANT!

If the behavior of both of your eyes doesn't improve, despite regular training in all areas, then I would advise you to consult a functional optometrist or a fully trained Neuro-Rider trainer in your local area or online. (You can find a list of all trainers at www.neuro-rider.com.)

Swap the target into your other hand.

Pass it over again at the bottom.

You can make a nice circle. Don't move your head!

EYE CIRCLES

Focus on: An easy drill for both eyes.

How to do it:
— Try a test.
— Start in Neutral Standing Position. Then pull your chin slightly down and back towards your Adam's apple, so your head tips very slightly forward. Hold your visual target in front of your body, around the height of your belly button, and focus on it.
— Move the pen in a circle. The diameter of the circle should be approximately the length of your lower arm. Work in "slow motion"—at least 10 seconds per revolution. Make sure you can see your target clearly every millisecond. Complete two to three revolutions in each direction.

Remember to breathe calmly!
— Retest, and record the results in the table. Repeat the drill with each eye individually.

TRAINING TIPS: EYE CIRCLES
— If you feel like your eyes jump or twitch in segments of the circular movement, then spend a little more time in these positions. You can do Gaze Stabilization, as well as mini-circles or small spirals in these positions. That should help.
— You can also do this drill with your weaker eye. Through the test-retest strategy, you can find out whether doing the drill with one eye is more effective for you.

Check your field of vision with a self-test.

PERIPHERAL VISION

Focus on: Perception of movement in the periphery. *Peripheral vision* is perhaps the most important visual function, and the one with the biggest influence on movement. We see things we aren't focusing on in our peripheral vision. Peripheral vision can take in a lot. We mainly perceive movements and shapes with our peripheral vision. We even have special cells for this purpose. When we're very stressed, our peripheral vision shrinks. That's where the expression "tunnel vision" comes from, and it isn't a state that helps with performance. When somebody is "in the tunnel" and their peripheral vision has shrunk, their chances of performing well are slim.

How to do it:
In my experience, athletes who train their peripheral vision respond less quickly and less strongly to stress stimuli—they remain calm and relaxed with a stable posture for longer, and as a result, they make fewer mistakes. Our field of vision is divided into four quadrants.

TRAINING OPTIONS
— The test as a drill.
— Training with the peripheral vision chart.
— Peripheral vision and walking.
— Peripheral vision and riding.
— Periphery-saccade chart.

For example, you could stand in front of a TV set, so you can see when the picture changes in your weaker field of vision. From this position you could train your Neuro-Rider moves and your peripheral vision at the same time.

It's easier with a coach.

Test the top right quadrant.

Focus on "X." Which letters can you identify without shifting your focus?

— Stand up straight and look at a point straight in front of you. Spread your arms out to the sides and start to slowly move your right hand forward from the back, while wiggling your fingers. Notice when you can perceive the movement of your hand in your field of vision.

— Leave your arm in the position where you saw the movement.

— Repeat the process with your other arm on the opposite side. Establish whether your field of vision is the same size on both sides. Repeat the test in the two upper quadrants and the two lower quadrants.

— Note in the table the differences in your right and left peripheral field of vision.

— If there are differences, stimulate the weaker side of your field of vision for one minute. If there are no differences, stimulate all the quadrants.

CAUTION!

Smaller differences of 10 to 20 degrees are usually unproblematic and harmless, and it should be possible to reduce them within a few minutes with a little practice. However, if you happen to notice at any point when you are practicing that there is a bigger difference, color changes, or one of the four quadrants is even missing, you should go to the hospital as soon as possible.

NEAR-FAR JUMPS

Focus on: Near-Far Jumps are easy to learn and to do. They train the accommodation movements of the eyes, in a similar way to the Cross-o-Matic (see p. 114)—only here, the eyes don't gently track, but rather quickly jump. This drill helps to balance out and regulate muscular tension. If you work a lot at a screen, this would be your first drill for a small screen training break—if your retest results are positive!

How to do it:
— Try a test.
— Start in Neutral Standing Position. Hold a visual target centrally in front of you, at eye level, very close to you, and focus on it—you don't need to be able to see it clearly. Then switch your focus quickly to a target at the same height but further away. You can use wall charts for vision tests as a visual target, but you can also just use your thumb as a "near" target, and a detail on a building or a tree in the distance as a "far" target. Switch back and forth between the targets for 30 seconds to a minute, switching to the other target as soon as you can see your current target clearly.
— Try to synchronize the rhythm of your breathing with your eye movement; breathe slowly and pause between each inhalation and exhalation.
— Retest, and record the results in the table.

ONE EYE OR BOTH EYES
You can also do this drill with your weaker eye. Through the test-retest strategy, you can find out whether doing the drill with one eye is more effective for you.

ACTIVATE YOUR BRAINSTEM
The muscle activation involved in near and distance vision activates different areas in the brainstem—with different effects on our muscle tone. The mid-brain helps the flexor muscles, and the pons increases the tone of the extensor muscles.

1

1 Near-Far Jumps in the stable as preparation.

2 Quick change of focus from very close ...

3 ... to far away. How quickly can you focus?

2

3

INHIBITION INSTEAD OF ACTIVATION

People who have suffered one or more concussions often show unusual responses during the Vision Drills. If you react sensitively to light and loud noises, this might also be the case for the these drills. You might retest badly on some of the drills. However, you might also feel unwell, become aggressive, or experience other emotional outbursts. These are normal responses to visual training. If you discover you have these tendencies, then here's some advice:

— Start with your Power Drills: Do a Power Drill before and after each Vision Drill.

— If possible, do one of your Power Drills or a Neutral Drill at the same time as you do a Vision Drill.

— Reduce the dose: Reduce the number of repetitions or the duration of the Vision Drills.

— Do a Breathing Drill first, ideally Air Hunger (see below), before a Vision Drill.

— Use the inhibition exercises I'll show you shortly. They make integration easier for the brain.

AIR HUNGER DRILLS

The areas that we want to relieve and at the same time indirectly train are in the midbrain. Air Hunger Drills activate neighboring areas and ensure more circulation in the areas that support the visual system (in this case, the *superior colliculus*). These areas should then work better. (See more about this on page 144.)

Glasses with holes. Very simple. Cheap pinhole glasses will do.

Looks cool, doesn't it?

PINHOLE GLASSES

Pinhole glasses reduce the amount of data your visual system has to process. This gives the visual system the chance to deal with a manageable quantity of data when it might otherwise be overwhelmed. Test and retest when using the pinhole glasses, as with any other drill. They're a new stimulus for the nervous system. I've seen clients put on pinhole glasses and be able to move their shoulders or bend their knees without pain for the first time in a year.

— Do your tests. Test how clearly you can see nearby objects. Wear the glasses for a minute and move around a little. Look around you. Retest to see whether your near vision has improved.

— Retest your Vision Drills afterward, with fewer repetitions, while you wear the glasses. If the retests are positive overall, then wear the pinhole glasses when you train. Start with two minutes. You can gradually wear them for longer. I can read or even watch TV wearing them, but please don't wear them for driving! Pinhole glasses are a nice, passive stimulus. All you have to do is wear them. You can also wear them for training other areas, and other drills might test and retest better as a result. Check it out.

Blue activates the nervous system.

COLORED GLASSES

The same goes for colored glasses. As surprising and strange as it might sound, we have receptors for red, green, and blue on our retinas. Accentuated stimulation of one category of receptors on the retina often leads to much better retests. Do what you did for the pinhole glasses. Test red, green, blue, and yellow (Ray, Fowler and Stein 2005). You can use all tests and retests for this.

BINASAL/UNINASAL PARTIAL OCCLUSION

Binasal Partial Occlusion is another cool drill and a great application that many people find extremely helpful and very cheap and easy to do. You can use Binasal Partial Occlusion in different ways. People usually use matte sticky tape, but nail polish or colored filters are equally effective. Stick the tape over the lenses of a pair of glasses, directly to the right and/or left of the nosepiece. You can experiment with the width

Green may have an effect on headaches and migraines.

of the strip to find out what's most effective for you.

Processing of visual information in the brain might be impaired after a fall and a concussion (but also after a stroke or brain tumor). The interruption of nerve fibers in the brainstem can have a negative effect on the balance and orientation systems.

Stick on two pieces of tape, approximately .5 inch (1 centimeter) wide...

... and this technique can also be used on normal glasses. Just give it a try.

In everyday life, people often feel overwhelmed in crowded areas such as shopping centers, parties, or warm-up areas.

The purpose of Binasal Partial Occlusion is to help with spatial orientation in these situations and others. Many of my athletes have benefited from it. A common response is that people feel more stable and safer when walking, running, performing, or riding. Binasal Partial Occlusion helps patients make better use of the (peripheral) visual system to keep track of their surroundings. Obviously, you can also stick something on your normal glasses. If you don't wear glasses, just buy a cheap pair without a prescription. You can safely wear the occlusion for several hours, and when riding or training. I have had successful experiences testing athletes with acute concussions, using this exercise. It's a great additional stimulus that doesn't take a lot of effort but can make an enormous difference for the right person. Test and retest—and give it a try on a horse.

EARPLUGS

What do earplugs have to do with vision? Well, people who are very sensitive to visual and/or acoustic stimuli have tissue in their midbrain in the area of the *inferior* and *superior colliculi* that, like a pulled muscle, isn't doing its job properly or isn't very healthy. The *superior colliculus* is where the first subconscious processing of visual information takes place, while the first rapid processing of acoustic information takes place in the *inferior colliculus*, situated directly below. These centers allow us to quickly react to these kinds of stimuli, as a reflex in case of danger, so they're an important part of our defense system. They control reflex-like neck movements and guide the eyes towards potential danger. But these areas can become overwhelmed. It can be helpful to reduce and/or modify incoming stimuli, and pinhole glasses, colored glasses, or even just earplugs are a very simple way of doing this.

— Try a test. Put ear plugs in one or both ears and move a little. Then retest each possibility individually, and use them in training accordingly. Record your results in the table.

— It's very possible that you'll be able to slowly increase your training scope in the visual area with earplugs and pinhole glasses. That's what we're aiming for. Look at it like a bandage for a knee injury—except in this case, the bandage is an earplug, and it isn't helping your knee, but your midbrain. Think of these drills as analogous to muscle training that would support that injured knee and promote healing.

ANXIETY

Pinhole or colored glasses and earplugs, coupled with Breathing Drills (physiological respiratory rhythm of ten seconds per breath) and combined with eye exercises, especially with either very fast Gaze Tracking or Cross-o-Matic and Near-Far Jumps (convergence/divergence drills), are good exercises for people who have problems with anxiety or panic attacks. They reduce stress via the vagus nerve (Bowan 2008). And since the eyes control movement, eye movements prepare us for what we would have to do to survive a real threat (fight or flight). Rapid eye movements like searching gaze jumps are a signal to the brain to act—to look for an escape, or to search for a weapon to protect yourself. These kinds of exercises tap into deeper, subcortical mechanisms that are below conscious thought. If you're struggling with inappropriate states of anxiety, it can be good to reduce your anxiety with these exercises. These drills can also help during acute panic attacks. However, you should practice them first so you can do them right if you need to.

Almost every household has some earplugs. We can use them to inhibit midbrain activation.

EXERCISES FOR THE VESTIBULAR SYSTEM
— *Well-Balanced!*

BALANCE AND EQUILIBRIUM

There's a little story I like to tell about a 60-year-old client who ended our telephone call with the words, "You're my last hope!" At our first meeting, she told me that she had pain all over her body.

A TEXTBOOK CASE

She had done far too little exercise over the last 10 years, and she was despairing because of the pain. Pressure at work, constant tension, and insomnia were all making her life hell. So far, nobody had been able to help her. No doctor, no physical therapist. All her vestibular tests were a catastrophic failure. Her proprioceptive abilities were very limited, she wasn't very good at precise movements, and even more significantly, she had no movement in her cervical spine.

I knew there was only a chance of change if the training began with visible success and the homework was easy. She needed vestibular activation, that was clear, but she simply couldn't do the drills correctly with the necessary precision and speed. I decided to test more non-specific drills instead of asking for precise and accurate movement and prescribed more of them. I taught her the Hourglass Exercise (p. 133), and we tested six repetitions—with much better results in retests.

I spent half an hour precisely and accurately teaching her the Hourglass. Her homework was to begin with six repetitions in the morning, and to do six repetitions in the parking lot every time she arrived somewhere: six at lunchtime, six in the afternoon, and six in the evening. She was to increase it to seven repetitions after a week. Then eight, then ten. We also talked about her diet. She said that she could easily drink a liter of orange juice a day. She also enjoyed roast liver, but hadn't eaten it for a long time. I sent her home with the Hourglass Drills, and a prescription for a liter of orange juice per day and one liver-based meal per week.

Because she had a long drive of two and half hours, I didn't see her again for six weeks. She was a completely different woman. Her pain had decreased from an "8" to a "1." After three weeks, she slept through the night again for the first time, and on the weekend, she'd had a lunchtime nap—which hadn't been possible until now. She told me she had to take a break after two days of training because she had muscle cramps, but that she started training again on the fourth day. She had tested six repetitions step by step and had worked her way up to 40. "I've lost 11 pounds," she told me, smiling. Now she wanted to learn to play tennis and wondered if I thought it was possible.

1

2

3

4

1 *The easiest standing position: feet shoulder-width apart.*

2 *Feet close together, or the "Romberg stance."*

3 *Feet together but not in line, or the "semi-tandem stance."*

4 *Feet in line, or the "tandem stance."*

STANDING POSITIONS

— Feet shoulder-width apart.
— Feet close together.
— Feet together but not in line.
— Feet in line, one behind the other.
— Standing on one leg.

It almost brought tears to my eyes. How could it be possible to achieve these changes so easily? We need to realize the vestibular system gives us guidance. It's important. It affects cognition, mobility, stress, sleep, even depression—basically our entire lives (Gurvich et al. 2013; Smith and Zheng 2013; Sailesh, Archana, and Mukkadan 2016). Orange juice counteracts inflammations in the intestine, and the sugar it contains counteracts the stress hormone cortisol. Liver is probably the most nutrient-rich food on earth. Lots of small things can come together to have a big effect.

START SIMPLE— THEN INTENSIFY

Some people need to reduce the difficulty and start off sitting with these drills, which is totally okay. However, most people start learning the drills in a Neutral Standing Position with the feet shoulder-width apart. You can increase the difficulty of the exercise by changing the standing position. This is therefore a way of modifying the dose. Remember – you must get the dose right! As your training progresses, you will be able to tolerate higher doses or maybe even need

Tests and Drills Vestibular System	on page	Neutral	Rehab	Power
Hourglass	130			
Giant Wheel with Gaze Stabilization	132			
Vestibulo-Ocular Reflex in Eight Directions	132			
To the top left				
To the left				
To the bottom left				
To the top right				
To the right				
To the bottom right				
Up				
Down				
Nodding "Yes" While Walking	135			
Nodding "No" While Walking	135			
Heel Bounces with Gaze Stabilization	136			
Head in a Neutral Position				
Head Tilted to the Right				
Head Tilted to the Left				
Figure Eights with Gaze Stabilization	136			

them, so you should increase the difficulty gradually so you can keep improving.

Train to your limit—keeping your balance is supposed to be difficult. It's okay to fail! Work from having your feet shoulder-width apart to keeping them close together, then to the offset stance, then to the tandem stance, and finally to standing on one leg. It's very difficult to do the drills standing on one leg. But when you have reached that point, you're guaranteed not to fall off your horse as easily.

HOURGLASS

Focus on: Stimulation for the vestibular system. This drill could also fit well into the Movement Drill category. I've included it here because it provides very good general stimulation for the vestibular system. After a few weeks of training, you should be able to manage as many Hourglass rotations as your age in years. If you do as many Hourglass Drills as your age in years every day, you'll continue to do very well for many years to come. And yes, you do one more every year! Unfortunately, the effort doesn't get any less as you get older.

Many people are familiar with classic "hip circles," but that's not what I'm talking about here. During hip circles, your head remains completely still, and as a result, the vestibular system is not activated through the *canals, sacculus,* and *utriculus*. This drill, however, kills two birds with one stone: it combines loads of input from the muscles of the spine and loads of input from the inner ear.

How to do it:
— Try a test.
— Start in Neutral Standing Position. Push your pelvis to the right while you tilt your spine to the left. From this point onward, your pelvis and upper spine always move in opposite directions.

— Your head moves forward and your pelvis moves back—in sync.
— Your head moves from the front to the right, and your pelvis moves from the back to the left.
— Your head moves back, your spine extends, and your pelvis pushes forward.
— Picture it: Draw circles on the ceiling with your head, and circles with your hips underneath. However, your head is always half a circle ahead (or half a circle behind, depending on how you look at it).
— Go slowly to begin with. Make sure your pelvis and head positions always move the same way in relation to each other and are opposite each other.
— Make sure your cervical and thoracic spine really extend, and your head doesn't stay in a neutral position. Your head needs to tilt in each direction—otherwise you won't activate the inner ear.
— Start with three revolutions in each direction. Did I already mention you should begin very slowly, in "slow motion"? And remember to breathe. It helps! Especially if you breathe in rhythm with the movement.
— Retest—but wait until any dizziness has passed. Record the results in the table.

TRAINING TIPS: HOURGLASS
— To begin with, it's easier if you focus on a spot slightly higher than eye level while you do the movement. You can allow your gaze to wander to the ceiling later.
— Dizzy? Have you done a positive test on one of the tongue positions (see p. 68)? Test whether maintaining one of these tongue positions while you perform the movement reduces your dizziness.
— If the retest results are bad, start with the other vestibular drills, and try this exercise again after three to four weeks of training.

1

2

3

4

5

6

7

1–3 Start with your feet shoulder-width apart, head and shoulders forward, and pelvis back, and then move the pelvis to the right, and the head to the left.

4–6 Circle your head and shoulders, and circle your pelvis. Both body parts should always be at precisely opposite points on the circle.

7 Let your arms relax and hang down. Do this exercise very carefully, starting in "slow motion" (see p. 42).

Giant Wheel: Start with your feet shoulder-width apart.

Keep looking at the weight.

Make the biggest circle you can.

GIANT WHEEL WITH GAZE STABILIZATION

This is a drill for stimulating the balance system and for strengthening the muscles of the upper body. You'll need a full 1.5-liter bottle of water, a small, lightweight kettle-bell, or something else that you can hold easily with two hands and move in a circle. A 13-pound (6-kilogram) kettlebell is being used in the photographs.

Focus on: The biggest circle possible, while keeping your gaze fixed on the target.

How to do it:
— Try a test.
— Start in Neutral Standing Position. Begin upright, with your gaze fixed on the weight. Now start drawing the biggest circle you can in front of you in the air, with your arms stretched out and the weight in your hands. Your eyes should be fixed on the weight while you make the circle. Bring the weight to the left and then up above your head with your arms stretched out as far as possible, then down to the ground and back up again to

the right, and then over your head again—always keeping your gaze and focus on a point on the weight. Begin with three to five revolutions in each direction.
— Retest. Wait a short time for any dizziness to pass. Record the results in the table.

VESTIBULO-OCULAR REFLEX IN EIGHT DIRECTIONS

Focus on: Rapid head rotations with gaze fixing in the most difficult standing positions. You might be asking yourself why you need so many different test directions. It's quite simple: Each head movement activates precisely one canal in the inner ear and inhibits the opposite partner in the canal. It might be the case that only one of your total of six canals requires activation—this can help deterimine that.

How to do it:
— Try a test.
— Start in Neutral Standing Position. Focus

Feel free to stretch up and over yourself.

Now downward; keep focusing on the target.

on a visual target approximately an arm's length in front of your eyes.

— Do a lightning-fast semi-rotation of your head to the right, keeping your eyes firmly on the target.

— At the end of the half "no," stop the movement, while still focusing on the target, and close your eyes. Count up to somewhere between 21 and 24 while bringing your head very slowly back to the center position with your eyes closed—very slowly, because otherwise you would activate the horizontal partner canal on the opposite side, and we want to achieve an isolated result for the right horizontal canal.

Back to the start, and continue.

— Open your eyes again, immediately focus on the target, and start from the beginning.

— Do around five repetitions as described.

— Retest. Move on to the next canal. Record the results in the table.

TRAINING TIPS

— If our vestibular system doesn't do its job well, then we won't manage to keep our eyes on the target consistently, or see it clearly. You'll notice this because your target will become blurred during the drill, or your eyes will move away from the target with your head.

— Reduce the speed of the head movement and keep practicing. If you find you're frequently unable to keep your eyes on the target, then you can use your tongue. Try the half "no" (p. 76); also test your tongue pressure in the left or right cheek (p. 68).

— If that helps, do more of it; if not try high frequency vibration via bone conduction headphones. You can find more information about them online.

THE EIGHT HEAD MOVEMENT DIRECTIONS FOR FORWARD
Here's a brief description of the other head movements.

01	To the upper left	Rapid head movement with your nose to the upper left—half extension and rotation.
02	To the left	Rapid head movement with your nose to the left—half extension and rotation.
03	To the bottom left	Rapid head movement with your nose to the bottom left—flexion and rotation, as if you wanted to send your right ear to the floor.
04	To the upper right	Rapid head movement with your nose to the top right—half extension and rotation.
05	To the right	See drill description on pp. 132-133.
06	To the bottom right	Rapid head movement with your nose to the bottom right—flexion and rotation, as if you wanted to send your left ear to the floor.
07	To the top	Rapid head movement with your nose to the top—extension, as if you were going to take a hook to the chin.
08	To the bottom	Rapid head movement with your nose to the bottom—flexion, as if you were a bull and wanted to move your horns into an attack position.

1 *2* *3* *4*

5 *6* *7* *8*

1 *2* *3* *4*

NODDING "YES" AND "NO" WITH GAZE STABILIZATION

Focus on: Head movements while alternating walking forward and backward. Sounds easy. Give it a try—but no staggering!

How to do it:
— Try a test.
— Hold a visual target at eye level in front of you, and focus on it. Start to walk, moving your head from left to right as if exaggeratedly shaking it to say "no," in a rotation, in rhythm with your steps, along the entire horizontal line. Move your head as much as in the rotation for the drill "Half No" (see p. 76). Walk forward 30 feet (10 meters), and then immediately change direction and walk 30 feet (10 meters) back again. Keep walking back and forth for one minute.

1–2 Walking with a change of direction, while shaking the head "no."
Variant: walking sideways.

3–4 Walking with a change of direction, while nodding the head "yes."
Variant: walking sideways.

— Retest. Repeat the process while nodding your head "yes" along the entire line. Record the results in the table.

FILM YOURSELF
Film yourself, or get someone else to film you doing a drill: Is your head rotation as clean as you learned it should be in the exercise on page 76? Are your steps getting bigger? Can you stay on the straight line, or do you start staggering?

HEEL BOUNCES WITH GAZE STABILIZATION

Focus on: Activation for the sacculus on both sides.

How to do it:
— Try a test.
— Start in Neutral Standing Position, this time with the knees straight.
— Focus on a fixed target on the wall—a box, bookshelves, a saddle, or similar—at eye level. Stand on tiptoe and let yourself rock back onto your heels, without absorbing the movement with your knee joints. Try to achieve a rapid frequency of successive bounces for 30 seconds.
— Retest. Record the results in the table.
— Repeat the process, both with your head tilted to the right and then with your head tilted to the left. Make sure you maintain the tilted positions consistently during the bounces.
— Retest. Record the results in the table.

FIGURE EIGHTS WITH GAZE STABILIZATION

Focus on: Keep going forward! This is a wonderful integrative exercise for several of your systems that can also be done while riding if it's working well on foot.

You will need a little space, two cones or similar, and a visual target. The ground markers/cones should be approximately 5 to 6 feet (2 meters) apart. The visual target should be at eye level on the wall approximately 5 to 6 feet (2 meters) away, in a central position. Your figure eight starts at the center point between the cones.

Heel bounces with a straight head position.

Head position tilted to the left.

Head position tilted to the right.

Figure eights look very easy, but...

... they are neurologically complex. The neck muscles,...

... the eyes, and the muscles of the spine have to ...

... work very well together.

How to do it:
— Try a test.
— Move forward around the cones in a figure eight, sticking close to them, without taking your eyes off the target on the wall and without touching the cones.
— Walk as fluidly and as quickly as you can for one minute.
— Retest. Record the results in the table.

MOVEMENT TIP
You will notice this drill isn't that easy. You should make sure you can see the cones in your peripheral vision—and then precisely match your stride length, speed, and the size of your turns to them. You need to precisely rotate your head and spine while your pelvis stays in line with the direction of movement.

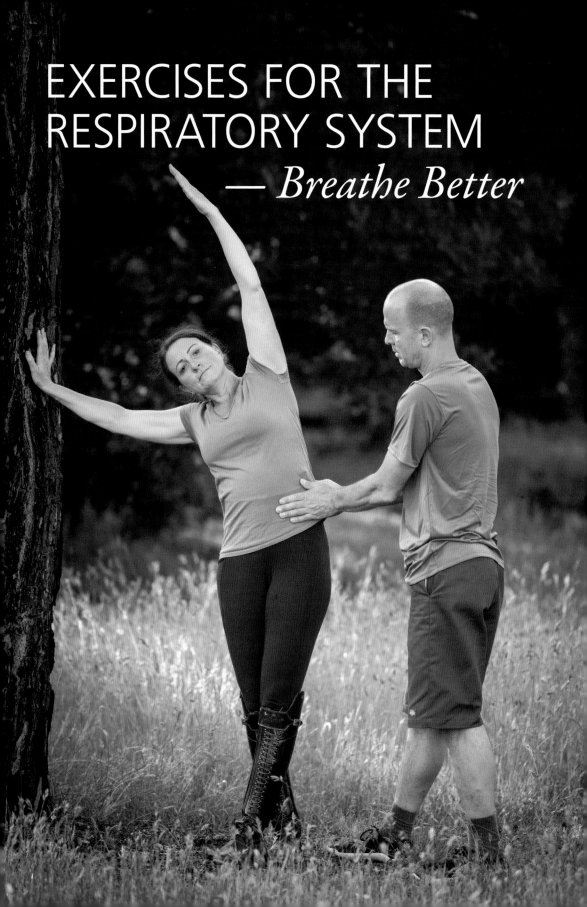

EXERCISES FOR THE RESPIRATORY SYSTEM
— *Breathe Better*

NEURO EXERCISES FOR YOUR RESPIRATORY SYSTEM

We take an average of 20,000 breaths per day. Many of us take too many breaths, thanks to stress, and breathe too frequently through our mouths. Many of us have experienced diseases involving our respiratory tracts, such as pneumonia, bronchitis, or COVID-19. And how many riders have never experienced bruised or fractured ribs?

PAY ATTENTION TO YOUR BREATHING

Stressors, including illnesses and injuries, change the mechanism, biomechanics, and habits of our breathing, and therefore also the oxygen supply to our brain, as a result of altered blood gas concentrations. Furthermore, active breathing is an excellent stimulus for many areas of the brain. Although the ancient yogis didn't know how their breathing techniques worked on a neuronal level, we now know why those techniques are so valuable.

BREATHING THROUGH A STRAW

Focus on: Count your breaths. You shouldn't do more than six complete breaths per minute.

How to do it:
— Try a test.
— Start in Neutral Standing Position. Breathe in through your nose for around three seconds and allow the air to escape through the straw. This will greatly reduce your respiratory rate. Don't force

High-tech equipment: Breathing through a straw.

Very helpful for stress and nerves.

139

Tests and Exercises Respiratory System	on page	Neutral	Rehab	Power
Breathing Through a Straw	139			
360-Degree Breathing	140			
Breathing with a Band	141			
Breathing Ladder	142			
Open Right				
Open Left				
Seated Dia-phragm Stretch	143			
Air Hunger	144			
Breathing into a Bag	145			

the air through the straw. Keep your breathing relaxed. It's normal to feel slight shortness of breath. Try not to react by breathing in more strongly.

— Keep going. Start with one minute and aim for 3 to 5 minutes.
— Retest, and record the results in the table.

360-DEGREE BREATHING

Focus on: Does your breath expand your ribcage in all directions?

How to do it:
— Try a test.
— Start in Neutral Standing Position. Firmly rub your upper body and your ribs with your hands. Stretch out your hands, and press them into your lower ribs at the sides so your thumbs cover your back ribs, and your fingers, your front ribs.
— Now breathe in slowly through your nose, and focus on expanding your rib cage evenly in all directions. Breathe in as far as

Sensory activation before the Breathing Drills...

... can be done by...

you can, and hold your breath—only for a short time, as long as you feel comfortable doing it—at the end of the inhalation, before breathing out slowly through your nose. Keep breathing like this for two to three minutes, which corresponds to approximately 10 slow breaths.

— Retest, and record the results in the table.

BREATHING WITH A BAND

Focal point: Careful breathing in and out with resistance. You will need a rubber band or a floss band (see www.neuro-rider.com).

— Try a test.

— Start in neutral standing position (page 70). Firmly rub your upper body and your ribs with your hands. Wrap the band once around your upper body, under your pectoral muscles. It should be tight enough that your rib cage feels some resistance when you breathe in.

— Now take a deep, even breath in through your nose. First, breathe into your abdomen, and try to evenly stretch the

Hand on your chest: Your breastbone should ...

... stay still when you breathe into your abdomen.

...rubbing the rib cage.

"Push your rib cage out."

Feel the even stretch.

141

"Generate movement under my hands."

"Generate movement through the breath."

rubber band in all directions—forward, to both sides, and to the back. Breathe out slowly through your nose. Hold your breath for as long as is comfortable at the end of each inhalation and exhalation. Breathe in this focused way for around two minutes.

— Retest, and record the results in the table.

BREATHING LADDER (OPEN LEFT)

Focus on: Generate movement in certain areas through your breath—first in isolation, then in sequence.

How to do it:
— Try a test.
— Start in Neutral Standing Position. Firmly rub the left side of your upper body, and your front and side ribs from top to bottom, with your hands. Bend your body far to the right, and use your right hand to support yourself against a

chair or wall. Stretch the area between your armpit and your iliac crest as much as possible on the side you are stretching.

— Place your right hand slightly above your right iliac crest. Your right side should be open and extended. Now begin to breathe in slowly through your nose, in the direction of your right hand. With a few breaths, try to expand your abdomen and the lower part of your back. We are talking about fractions of an inch, and about paying attention to this area. The actual expansion is secondary.

— Breathe calmly and slowly through your nose, and focus on expanding the area where your right ribs begin, alternating between the front and the back. Spend some time exploring this area and find appropriate control.

— Now consciously breathe into your shoulders only. Expand your upper rib cage; your clavicle should lift slightly, along with your shoulder blades. Keep your focus here for a few breaths.

— Now join up all the stages evenly in one

breath. Breathe in and out. Do two or three coordinated, even breaths, very slowly.

— Retest, record the results in the table, and then repeat the breath ladder on the other side and retest again.

SEATED DIAPHRAGM STRETCH

Focus on: Regaining full control over your breath, and breathing calmly two breaths after Air Hunger (see next page).

— Try a test.
— Sit up straight on a chair. Lace your fingers behind your head and pull your elbows back, with your neck extended.

Open your mouth and exhale all the air in your lungs in one single drawn-out breath. The fun only really begins when you think all your breath is gone, because there will still be a few more cubic inches of mixed air in your lungs—and you need to get rid of that, too. Squeeze, squeeze, squeeze. Use all of the muscles that can help. Keep your arms behind your head! You might find you have to wheeze or whistle, or your ribs feel cramped. This is normal. You will regret smoking those last Marlboros, but no problem. Give it a try. Believe in yourself!

— When you've finished the maximum exhalation, close your mouth and hold

In a seated position, straighten your pelvis, ...

... link your arms behind your head, ...

... pull your elbows back, ...

... extend your neck, open your mouth—and squeeze.

Air Hunger? Child's play!

DON'T JUST GIVE UP!
This drill can cause cramps or trigger coughing fits. I promise you it will get better. If you need to, approach it slowly, step-by-step. Favor the other drills, but keep coming back to the diaphragm stretch. It's worth it. This drill might feel terrible to begin with, but it conceals pure gold, and you'll learn to love it.

your breath. Now there's almost a vacuum in your lungs. You should be sitting in a hunched position. Completely relax your abdomen. Slowly straighten up from this position, extending your spine.

— Your abdominal cavity should be pulled in. Now relax your throat, and let the air flow back into your lungs in one go.

— Take a break of approximately 20 seconds and start again. Do three to six repetitions.

— Retest, and record the results in the table.

AIR HUNGER

Focus on: Control and hold your breath.

How to do it:
Try a test.

— Relax and exhale almost completely. Now do any kind of neutral physical activity that you know won't have any influence on your retest: walking, squats, vacuuming, climbing the stairs—whatever. All that matters is that your muscles produce carbon dioxide and that you don't exhale this carbon dioxide. Hold your breath for as long as possible while you move. When it gets uncomfortable and the inhalation reflex kicks in, and you start to feel like you need to breathe in, then you can breathe in again.

You don't necessarily have to cover your mouth and nose.

STICK WITH IT!
No, this drill isn't very pleasant—but it's worth it. Do the Air Hunger Drill several times a day for three weeks, and your fitness level will increase exponentially without any stamina training.

Put the bag over your mouth and nose.

Relax and breathe into the bag.

Take a breath of fresh air if you need to.

— *But* don't take a massive, uncontrolled in-breath like a half-dead sprinter at the finish line. Take a maximum of three normal breaths—then you should be able to have a relaxed conversation again.

— Firstly, it's about increasing the CO_2 content of your blood, and calibrating your pH receptors to the idea that higher CO_2 levels are great, and secondly, it's about maintaining cognitive control over your breath and learning that oxygen deficiency problems don't occur very quickly in halfway healthy people.

— Retest, and record the results in the table.

BREATHING INTO A BAG

Focus on: To increase the CO_2 content in the air you're breathing.

You'll need a bag. It should preferably be made of paper, but it doesn't have to be. This is the easiest drill you can do to increase the CO_2 in your blood and therefore the amount of oxygen released into your tissues (search for the "Bohr effect" and "Haldane effect").

How to do it:

Try a test.

— Breathe into the bag. The edges of the bag don't have to form an airtight seal around your nose and mouth, because then the drill would be over very quickly. The aim is simply to inhale a gas mixture from the bag that has more carbon dioxide in it than the air outside the bag. Relaxation normally occurs quickly. Calmly breathe the carbon-dioxide-enriched air in through your nose and slowly back out for 3 to 4 minutes.

— Retest, and record the results in the table.

PREVENTING PANIC

Breathing into a bag is a classic remedy for panic attacks. The effect can be intensified if you do Vision Drills such as Near-Far Jumps (p. 120) or Saccades (p. 110) at the same time. This drill is also ideal for breaks between sets during training. Or generally as a way of calming down. Or quite simply to warm up your hands and feet—if previous excessive breathing through stress or similar was the cause...

NEURO-RIDER TRAINING

— Questions and Answers

SHAPING YOUR NEURO-RIDER TRAINING

Congratulations! You have now taken the first step; you've learned about testing and retesting, and familiarized yourself with all the drills. What now? Here are a few suggestions for how to integrate Neuro-Rider Training into your everyday life, and how you can train regularly.

HOW LONG, HOW OFTEN, HOW MUCH?

You are now familiar with testing and re-testing, and you've hopefully already learned something about your body and your brain. The answers to the questions above are simple: You decide. Don't overdo it, because that's demotivating. Do one exercise per day. Make it a long-term project. Do a few minutes every day. If you have more time, do more. Fun is important. You should learn to love training, because it makes you better! So relax—and have a little fun with it!

If you want to do it the hard way, and know that you can cope with it: Practice two to six times every day for 5 to 15 minutes. Set yourself up so the commitment is realistic for you in terms of time. Give yourself one day off training a week.

Plan the sessions so you do them not just on a good day, but on a day when everything is going wrong—you know what I mean.

One rule: Never miss it twice. You can always end up missing a day's training; shit happens. But try really hard to never completely skip training on two consecutive days. At least try to always do some of your Power Drills before sitting on a horse.

THE LAISSEZ-FAIRE APPROACH

Start by only training your Power Drills.

Do them whenever you feel like it: after getting up, after breakfast, in short breaks from work, before an important meeting, as a mini-break from the screen, to prepare for your riding lesson, at the barn, when leading your horse, before getting on, as a break to recalibrate yourself during a riding lesson, to relax in the evening, or as a long sequence when you've got half an hour free. Anything is possible, and however it fits into your life is good.

Make sure you do a few minutes of Power Drills every day, but obviously you can do more.

You should incorporate a longer session every four to eight weeks; test and retest all the drills again, and update your set of training drills accordingly.

Training on horseback.

Peripheral vision and Saccades.

You should only transfer an exercise to "on-horse" when the exercise is working "off-horse."

Better neuronal basics ...

... let you finally achieve a pirouette.

THE ALL-IN APPROACH

For the next six weeks, train exclusively with your Power Drills. Try to practice for 10 to 30 minutes every day. It doesn't matter whether you do your training in one go or in several shorter sessions.

After six to eight weeks, test all the drills again and see whether the Rehab Drills from the first testing have begun to rehabilitate themselves. If you're lucky, there will now be a few less of them.

Then continue training, but always add three or a maximum of four Rehab Drills each week. Do the Rehab Drills either according to the *Hamburger Principle* or the *Combining Principle*.

The Hamburger Principle works like this: Do a Power Drill, and then immediately afterward a Rehab Drill, followed by a Power Drill. (Easy.)

The Combining Principle saves time, but it can be a little more complicated and doesn't always work for all drills: Combine a Rehab Drill with a Power Drill. If none of your Power Drills are suitable for combining, then add a suitable Neutral Drill you can do well. Make sure you finish each mini training session with a Power Drill. You should be better after every training session than you were before.

PS: The sentence above might be short and simple, but that doesn't mean it isn't important. So here it is again in bold: **You should be better after every training session than you were before.**

After six more weeks at the latest, you should have cleared most rehab drills. Then it's time for the next ones—if there are any. Now it's time for a piece of extremely important advice.

BE YOUR OWN BIGGEST FAN—SUSTAINABLE LEARNING AND TRAINING

To learn all the drills in this book so well you could do them in your sleep requires a few factors I'd like to discuss with you now:
— Frequency
— Attention
— Novelty

FREQUENCY

If you want to ride better, you will need a certain amount of regular repetition. No athlete can do without it. You need to keep reminding your brain you want to ride better. If you don't incorporate these drills regularly into your everyday life, then your brain will think you don't have any interest in retaining and preserving what it has learned.

ATTENTION

Attention is the basic currency for learning. The best athletes in the world train without the distraction of their mobile phone or their partner, and consistently avoid interruptions. It's nice to have a chat—but only when you're taking a break, not while you're in the middle of training. Your brain needs to be ready to make a few serious changes.

NOVELTY

Some Power Drills could lose a little of their magic after a few weeks of training. If that happens, then it's time to incorporate some novelty into your training, and maybe increase the difficulty. You can also increase your level of attention again by:
— Changing your posture—try altering the position of one of your joints.
— Choosing a more difficult standing position.

1

2

3

4

Neuro-Rider Training also includes:

1 & 2 *Sensory testing and activation.*

3   *Testing two-point discrimination.*

4   *Saccades combined with hand movement*
      with rhythm.

5   *The more stable the rider's spine is, the easier*
      it is for the horse to keep his neck straight.

5

— Do the drills using different compass lunge variations (see below).
— Change your eye position when doing movement drills.
— Rotate your upper body or head to the right or left.
— Do the drills very precisely, to the rhythm of a metronome or to music.
— Change and play with your breathing rhythm.
— Train in different places.
— If possible, do the exercises on a horse.

INCREASE THE LEVEL OF DIFFICULTY

EXAMPLE: COMPASS LUNGE VARIATIONS

If you want to keep improving, you need to make your training more difficult over time. It needs to be challenging enough for you to really have to push yourself to do the exercises cleanly and with stability.

For example, you can use the five different lunge positions to do the drills on a wider (standing) base, and to train all the movements in different load situations. If you can do all the drills in a Neutral Standing Position, you can increase the difficulty according to your performance level by practicing the same drills in lunge positions. You can simply start by practicing "straighten and tilt pelvis" in all 10 lunge positions. You'll be surprised how different the feeling of control is in these positions. Don't forget to test and retest.

QUESTIONS ARE GOOD!

START TRAINING AND THEN ASK QUESTIONS

WILL I IMPROVE WITH FIVE MINUTES A DAY?

Yes. If you haven't done any training, and you start training for just one minute, that's an increase of 100%. You'll feel better, and you'll ride better, too. You'll really enjoy experimenting with the drills and transferring them to riding. And maybe you'll slowly start doing more of them, just because you want to. Make training a habit. Reward

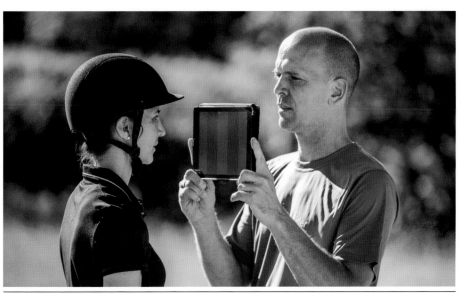

Optokinetic reflex stimulation.

Rolling a tennis ball along the thoracic spine while on horseback—but please learn and test this "off-horse" first!

yourself for your successes. Imagine you trained for one minute longer every week. After one year, that would be 52 minutes. That's how training works: slowly. Baby steps can be powerful if you keep taking them. Make a habit of it!

I ALREADY TRAIN AT THE GYM. CAN I COMBINE THIS WITH NEURO-RIDER TRAINING?

Definitely. Use the drills as a warmup or as direct preparation for strength exercises. Important: Apply the principles you've learned, such as the test-retest strategy, to check your overall training and each one of your exercises in the gym. Let go of everything that makes you worse. Do more of what makes you better. Then things will really start happening! Do it!

MY RETESTS ARE QUICKLY BECOMING WORSE AND LESS CONSISTENT. WHAT AM I DOING WRONG?

Nothing. Metabolism is usually the problem here. Focus on breathing drills for two to three weeks, and do many more of them. Do as many as you can. Drink at least 1 liter of orange juice per day; sugar increases carbon dioxide. Make sure you're getting enough protein. Then try it again!

DOES IT MATTER WHETHER I TRAIN ONCE A DAY FOR 20 MINUTES OR FOUR TIMES A DAY FOR FIVE MINUTES?

No, it doesn't. Whatever fits better into your life. I like to train for 20 sessions of 1 minute per day, but sometimes I only train for five sessions of 1 minute. What matters most is that I do it every day. From time to time, I like to train for longer. I love it.

I'M A BIT OF A PERFECTIONIST. WHAT WOULD BE OPTIMAL FROM A SCIENTIFIC POINT OF VIEW?

There's hardly any data, and each person is different. Unfortunately, I don't know you. Experiment. To achieve lasting changes in the brain, you need 20 to 40 hours of targeted, strong stimuli. And that's not including breaks! 20 hours is for people who have a good metabolism; it'll take longer if your metabolism has been damaged through training, malnutrition, or illness. Do what makes you better.

ISN'T THERE ANY EMPIRICAL DATA?

There is. If people train in a focused manner for 15 minutes every day, the first cool CIB experiences (see p. 11) will come after around six weeks. Their results will often have dramatically improved after 12 weeks. You do the math: That's 22.5 hours of training in 12 weeks. But some people need twice as long, while others need to heal their metabolism first before change is possible.

KEYWORD: NUTRITION. HOW CAN I IMPROVE MY METABOLISM?

This question is worthy of a couple of doctoral theses. Let's start with a simple answer: test-retest strategy. Test: Measure your basal body temperature and take your pulse in bed in the morning before you get up. Anything that raises your body temperature and your pulse is good. Do more of it. I give online seminars about this now and then.

Happy brain—happy rider—happy horse!

FINAL WORDS

This book is a useful aid for beginning your training, and shows how you can get started in the extensive repertoire of Neuro-Rider Training. It's a good jumping-off point. But we know that getting started isn't always easy. You might have started training, but something got in the way, and you didn't continue. Did you know that most people need more than eight attempts to get used to a new behavior such as regular training? I find that comforting. It also shows that failure is normal. No problem. But before starting again, it's worthwhile to analyze how and when you can organize your training differently and make a new, better plan.

    All the best—have fun, and happy riding!

INDEX

Page numbers in *italics* refer to figures and photographs.

A

Air Hunger, 121, 144–145, *144*

All-in approach, 149

Ankle drills, 98–100, *98–100*

Anxiety

Breathing Drills for, 26, 145

neuromatrix for, 24

perception of threats and, 22–26

Vision Drills for, 125

Articular effusions, 39

Attention, 149

Autonomic nervous system, 83

Ayres, Anna Jean, 33

B

Backward Hip Circles, 96–97, *96*

Balance and equilibrium training, 55–60, 126–137

background, 33–34, 55, 127–129

case study, 127–129

effective dose, 129–130

Gaze Stabilization with Figure Eights, *31*, 136–137, *137*

Gaze Stabilization with Giant Wheels, 132, *132–133*

Gaze Stabilization with Nodding "Yes" and "No," 135, *135*

Heel Bounces with Gaze Stabilization, 136, *136*

Hourglass Drill, *26–27*, 127, 130, *131*

lumbar spine circles as, 86, *86–88*, 88

standing positions, 128, *128*

Test–Drill–Retest drills, 55–60

Vestibulo-Ocular Reflex in Eight Directions, 132–134, *134*

Walk the Line, 49, 59, *59*

worksheet, 129

Zombie Stand, 49, 55, 56–57, *56*

Zombie Stand variations, 57–59, *57–58*

Balance issues, as brake booster, 21, 33

Basal body temperature, 153

Basal ganglia, 38

Basic training, 41

Before-and-after comparisons, 40

Bend Your Thoracic Spine in a Sideways Position, 85, *85*

Binasal/Uninasal Partial Occlusion, 123–124, *124*

Blood sugar levels, 18, 21

Bone conduction headphones, 133

Brain activity patterns, 45

Brain function. *See* Neuro-rider training

Brainstem, 34, 111, 120, 123

Brakes (releasing threats), 18–21

Breathing drills, 138–145

Air Hunger, 121, 144–145, *144*

for anxiety, 26, 145

background, 36–38, 139

Breathing into a Bag, 145, *145*

Breathing Ladder (Open Left), 142–143, *142*

Breathing Through a Straw, 139–140, *139*

Breathing with a Band, 141–142, *141*

drills, 139–145

for pain and anxiety, 26, 145

Seated Diaphragm Stretch, *38*, 143–144, *143*

360-Degree Breathing, 140–141, *140–141*

worksheet, 140

Breathing into a Bag, 145, *145*

Breathing Ladder (Open Left), 142–143, *142*

Breathing Through a Straw, 139–140, *139*

Breathing with a Band, 141–142, *141*

Bubka, Sergey, 41

C

Canals of vestibular system, *33*, *34*, 130, 132

Carbon dioxide, 38, 144–145, 152

Central cerebellum, 65, 107

Cerebellum, *11*

coordination and, 59–60, 111, 113

gaze stabilization and, 107

tongue movement and, 65

voluntary breathing and, 38

Cervical spine drills, 72–82, *73–82*

Cervical spine issues, 104

CIB effects, 11–12, 26, 32, 153

Ciliary muscles, 104

Classical training comparison, 11

Colored glasses, 123, *123*, 124–125

Combining Principle, 149

Compass lunge variations, 151

Concussions, 5–6, 114, 121

Contraindications, 39–40

Convergence drills, 114, 125

Convergence insufficiency, 115

Coordination test, 59–60, *60*

Cortisol, 129

Costal pleura, 37

Cost/benefit ratio, 43, *43*

Could It Be? (CIB) questions, 11–12, 26, 32, 153

Cranial nerves, 83, 104, 115

Cross-Body Hip Circles, 95–96, *95*

Cross-Body Shoulder Circles, 92–93, *92*

Cross-o-Matic (Pencil Press-Up), 114–115, *114*, *116*, 125

D

Diaphragm, 36–37, *36–38*

Diaphragm stretch, *38*, 143–144, *143*

Divergence drills, 114, 125

Drill, defined, 48. *See also* Test–Drill–Retest

Dura mater (outer meninges), 37, 83

E

Earplugs, 124–125

Effective dose, 43, *43*

Equilibrium drills. *See* Balance and equilibrium training

Equilibrium issues, 21, 33

Execution perfection, 41

Exercises. *See* Balance and equilibrium training; Breathing drills; Physical awareness drills; Test–Drill–Retest (drills); Vision drills

Eye Circles, 117–118, *117*

Eye movement dysfunctions, 18–19

F

Fast speed, 42, *42*

Fear of heights, 23–24

Figure Eights with Gaze Stabilization, *31*, 136–137, *137*

Figure Eights with the Hands, 91, *91*

Flexibility tests, 51–56

background, 51

Forward Bend, 49, 51, *51*

Half Snow Angel (Shoulder Abduction), 53, *53*

Pistol Rotation (Full Body Rotation), 28–29, 49, 54–56, *55*

Scarecrow (Inward and Outward Shoulder Rotation), 52–53, *52*

Shoulder Flexion, 54, *54*

Flexion and Extension of the Cervical Spine (Yes-Yes Movement), 78, *78*

Forward Bend (Hip Flexion), 49, 51, *51*

Forward Hip Circles, 94–95, *95*

Forward Shoulder Circles, 92, *92*

Fractures, 19, 39

"Frame of reference that brings everything together," 33. *See also* Balance and equilibrium training

Frequency of training, 149

Frontal lobes, *11*, 14, 37, 111, 113

Fuel for the brain, 18, 38, 45, 108, 127, 129, 152

Full Body Rotation (Pistol Rotation), *28–29*, 49, 54–56, *55*

Fun factor, 40

G

Gait pattern, 61–62

Gaze Stabilization in Nine Points, *106*, 107–108

Gaze Stabilization with Figure Eights, *31*, 136–137, *137*

Gaze Stabilization with Giant Wheel, 132, *132–133*

Gaze Stabilization with Heel Bounces, 136, *136*

Gaze Stabilization with Nodding "Yes" and "No," 135, *135*

Gentle Gaze Tracking in Eight Directions, 108–110, *108–109*, 112, 113, 125

Giant Wheel with Gaze Stabilization, 132, *132–133*

Glasses (colored), 123, *123*, 124–125

Glasses (pinhole), 122–123, *122*, 124–125

Glasses (prescription), 103–104

Glide Back and Forth in a Sideways Position (The Hen in a Sideways Position), 82, *82*, 83

Glide the Cervical Spine Back and Forth (The Hen), 80, *80*, 83

Glide the Flexed Cervical Spine Back-and-Forth (The Pecking Hen), 80–81, *81*, 83

Glucose, 18, 45, 103, 108

Goal setting, 40

Gravitation, perception of, 34

H

Half No (Rotation of the Cervical Spine), *76–77*, *76–77*, 133, 135

Half Snow Angel (Shoulder Abduction), 53, *53*

Hamburger Principle, 149

Hand RAPS, 59–60, *60*, 111, 112

Hanna, Thomas, 27

Heel Bounces with Gaze Stabilization, 136, *136*

The Hen (Glide the Cervical Spine Back and Forth), 80, *80*, 83

The Hen in a Sideways Position (Glide Back and Forth in a Sideways Position), 82, *82*, 83

Hip Circles in Four Positions, 94–97, *94–96*

Hip Flexion (Forward Bend), 49, 51, *51*

Hourglass Drill, *26–27*, 127, 130, *131*

How long, how often, how much? 43, 147–153

Hypermetric Saccades, 111

Hypometric Saccades, 111

I

"I don't like it, but it was still good" drill, 62, *62–63*

Inferior colliculus, 124

Inflammation, 39

Inhibition, instead of inactivation, 121

Injuries, as brake booster, 19

Input (receptors for brain)
background, 12–14, *13*
from joints, 19, 28–29
perception of safety and, 16–17, *16*
principles for, 17
survival reflexes and, 14–16, *14–15*, 24
of vestibular system, 34

Insular cortex, 38

Intensified Zombie Stand, 57, *57*

"In the tunnel," 118

Inward and Outward Shoulder Rotation (Scarecrow), 52–53, *52*

Isometric Full Body Contraction, 100–101, *101*

Isometric training, 72–83, 100–101, *101*

J

Joint hypermobility, 39

Joint inflammation, 39

Joint issues, 19, 28–29

Joint mobilization, 28–29, 39. *See also* Physical awareness drills

Joint replacements, 39

K

Knee Circles, 97–98, *97*

L

Laissez-faire approach, 147

Lateral Flexion of the Cervical Spine, 79, *79*

LeDoux, Joseph, 23

Liver, 127, 129

Lumbar Spine in a Semicircle Backward, 88, *88*

Lumbar Spine in a Semicircle Forward, 86, *86–87*

M

Macular organs, 34

Malignant tumors, 39

Masterful movement, 41

Measurable goals, 40

Mechanoreceptors, 19, 28–29

Metabolism, 152, 153

Midbrain, 104

Mittelstädt, Hans, 34

Moseley, Lorimer, 23

Motor cortex, 38, 45

Movements. *See* Balance and equilibrium training; Breathing drills; Physical awareness drills; Test–Drill–Retest (drills); Vision drills

N

Near-Far Jumps, 120, *120–121*, 125, 145

Neck isometry, 72–83

Nervous system, test–drill–retest principle for, 47

Nervus oculomotorius, 104

Neuromatrix, 24

Neuroplasticity, 45

Neuro-rider training, 4–45

    activation of, 43–45

    for anxiety and pain alleviation, 22–26, 125, 145

    brain function overview, *11*, 12–14, *13*

    CIB effects, 11–12, 26, 32, 153

    classical training comparison, 11

    concussions and, 5–6, 114, 121

    contraindications for, 39–40

    final words, 153

    foundation for, 10, 46–63. *See also* Test–Drill–Retest

    goal setting, 40

    on-horse work, *22*, *44*, *148*, *152*

    how long, how often, how much? 43, 147–153

    importance of, 5

    inputs and outputs, 12–14, *14–15*. *See also* Input; Output

    objectives, 8, 11

    personalization of, 8–10

    preparation for, 40–45

    for proprioception system, 26–29, 64–101. *See also* Physical awareness drills

    purpose of, 3

    questions and answers, 43, 147–153

    releasing threats (brakes), 18–21

    for respiratory system, 36–38, 138–145. *See also* Breathing drills safety perception and, 16–21, *16. See also* Safety

survival reflexes, 14–16, *14–15*, 24

training to ride, 5, 11

for vestibular system, 33–34, 126–137. *See also* Balance and equilibrium training

for visual system, 30–32, 102–125. *See also* Vision drills

Neutral Drill, 62, *63*, 104

Neutral Standing Position with the Spine Long, 70–72, *71*

Nodding "Yes" and "No" with Gaze Stabilization, 135, *135*

Nölke, Marc, *1–2*, 2–3, 5

Novelty, 149

O

Occipital cortex, 30

Old injuries, as brake booster, 19

One-Eyed Cross-o-Matic, 115, *116*

One-legged Zombie Stand, 57, 58–59, *58*

On-horse work, *22*, 44, 148, 152

Open Left (Breathing Ladder), 142–143, *142*

OptoDrum (optokinetic app), 112–113, *112–113*, 151

Optokinetic nystagmus, 112

Optokinetics, 112, *112-113*

Orange juice, 45, 108, 127, 129, 152

Outer meninges (dura mater), 37, 83

Output (brain)

anxiety and pain as, 23

background, 12–14, *13*

perception of safety and, 16–17, *16*

principles for, 17

survival reflexes and, 14–16, *14–15*, 24

Oxygen supply, 18, 38, 45

P

Padula, William, 30, 32

Pain

background, 22–26

case study, 127–129

neuromatrix for, 24

perception of threats and, 17, 22–26

Panic attacks, 125, 145

Parietal lobes, 45, 113

Parkinson's disease, 5–6

The Pecking Hen (Glide the Flexed Cervical Spine Back-and-Forth), 80–81, *81*, 83

Pelvic floor, 37

Pelvic position, 89

Pelvic Rotations, 90, *90*

Pencil Press-Up (Cross-o-Matic), 114–115, *114, 116*, 125

Perception of safety, 16–21, *16–17*

Perfect execution, 41

Pericardium, 37

Peripheral vision, 32

Peripheral vision training, 118–119, *118–119*, 137

Personalization of training, 8–10

Physical awareness drills, 64–101

background, 26–29, 65–66

Bend and Stretch the Thoracic Spine, 83–84, *83–84*

Bend Your Thoracic Spine in a Sideways Position, 85, *85*

Cross-Body Shoulder Circles, 92–93, *92*

Figure Eights with the Hands, 91, *91*

Forward Shoulder Circles, 92, *92*

Half No, 76–77, *76–77*

The Hen, 80, *80*, 83

The Hen in a Sideways Position, 82, *82*, 83

Hip Circles in Four Positions, 94–97, *94–96*

Isometric Full Body Contraction, 100–101, *101*

Knee Circles, 97–98, *97*

Lateral Flexion of the Cervical Spine, 79, *79*

Lumbar Spine in a Semicircle Backward, 88, *88*

Lumbar Spine in a Semicircle Forward, 86, *86–87*

Neutral Standing Position with the Spine Long, 70–72, *71*

The Pecking Hen, 80–81, *81*, 83

Pelvic Rotations, 90, *90*

Pull Toes Out, 100, *100*

Pull Toes Straight, 99, *99*

Push the Head Back, 74, *74*

Push the Head Forward, 72–73, *73*

Push the Head to the Left, 74–75, *74–75*

Push the Head to the Right, 75, *75*

Side Shoulder Circles, 93, *93*

Straighten and Tilt Pelvis, 89, *89*

Tilt Ankle Outward, 98, *98*

tongue drills, 65–69, *68–69*

Vibration on the Teeth, 70, *70*

worksheet, 67

Yes-Yes Movement, 78, *78*

Pinhole glasses, 122–123, *122*, 124–125

Pistol Rotation (Full Body Rotation), *28–29*, 49, 54–56, *55*

Post-operative recovery period, 39

Power Drill, 62, *62*, *63*, 147, 149–151

Preparation for training, 40–45

Prescription glasses, 103–104

Press the Tongue into Right and Left Cheek, 68–69, *69*, 133

Processing input (brain)
    background, 12–14, *13*
    perception of safety and, 16–17, *16*
    principles for, 17
    survival reflexes and, 14–16, *14–15*, 24

Proprioception
    background, 26–29
    exercises for, 55–60, 64–101. *See also* Physical awareness drills
    vestibular system and, 34

Psoas, 37

Pull Toes Out, 100, *100*

Pull Toes Straight, 99, *99*

Push the Head Back, 74, *74*

Push the Head Forward, 72–73, *73*

Push the Head to the Left, 74–75, *74–75*

Push the Head to the Right, 75, *75*

R

Rapid Alternating Pronation and Supination (Hand RAPS), 59–60, *60*

Reflexes for survival, 14–16, *14–15*, 24

Rehab Drill, 62, *63*

Rehab Movement Drill with a Power Eye Position, 107–108

Rehab Position in the Hip, 94, *94*

Relaxed nasal breathing, 26

Releasing threats (brakes), 18–21

Respiratory issues, as brake booster, 18

Respiratory system, 36–38, 139–145. *See also* Breathing drills

Retest, defined, 48. *See also* Test–Drill–Retest

Riding simulator, *44*

Romberg stance, *128*

Rotation of the Cervical Spine (Half No), 76–77, *76–77*, 133, 135

S

Saccades, 110–111, *110*, 112–113, 145

Saccule (sacculus), *33*, 34, 130, 136

Safety
    perception of, 16–17, *16*
    releasing threats (brakes), 18–21
    survival reflexes and, 14–16, *14–15*, 24

Sagittal suture, of skull, 83

Salazar, Zachariah, 9

Scalene muscles, 37

Scarecrow (Inward and Outward Shoulder Rotation), 52–53, *52*

Sea sickness, 34

Semi-tandem stance, *128*

Sensory cortex, 45

Sensory Integration and the Child (Ayres), 33

Sensory motor amnesia, 27

Shoulder Abduction (Half Snow Angel), 53, *53*

Shoulder drills, 52–54, *52–54*, 92–93, *92–93*

Shoulder Flexion, 54, *54*

Side Shoulder Circles, 93, *93*

Sideways Hip Circles, 96, *96*

Sit-ups, 83

Skull suture, 83

Sleep issues, 21, 127

Slow speed, 42, *42*

Social problems, as brake booster, 21

Somatic graviception, 34

Speed of movements, 42, *42*

Sternocleidomastoid muscle, 72

Straighten and Tilt Pelvis, 89, *89*

Stress, as brake booster, 21. *See also* Anxiety

Superior colliculus, 30, 121, 124

Supplementary motor area, 37

Survival reflexes, 14–16, *14–15*, 24

T

Tandem stance, *128*

Test, defined, 48

Test–Drill–Retest (general)

    background, 47–49

    balance tests, 55–60

    categorization of drills, 62–63, *62–63*

    coordination test, 59–60

    defined, 48

    flexibility tests, 51–56

    other movements as tests and retests, 61–62

    pain scale for, 61, *61*

    as part of training, 63

    worksheet, 50

Test–Drill–Retest drills

    Forward Bend (Hip Flexion), 49, 51, *51*

    Half Snow Angel (Shoulder Abduction), 53, *53*

    Hand RAPS, 59–60, *60*

    Pistol Rotation (full body rotation), *28–29*, 49, 54–56, *55*

    Scarecrow (Inward and Outward Shoulder Rotation), 52–53, *52*

    Shoulder Flexion, 54, *54*

    Walk the Line, 49, 59, *59*

    Zombie Stand, 49, 55, 56–57, *56*

    Zombie Stand variations, 57–59, *57–58*

Thalamus, 30

Thoracic spine drills, 83–85, *83–85*

Thoracic spine problems, 104

360-Degree Breathing, 140–141, *140–141*

Tilt Ankle Outward, 98, *98*

Tongue Circles with the Mouth Closed, 68, *69*

Tongue in Resting Position, Fake Smile, and Swallow drill, 68, *69*, 130

Tongue Press into Right and Left Cheek, 68–69, *69*, 133

Tongue Stretch, 69, *69*

Torn ligaments, as brake booster, 19

Total joint replacement, 39

Training to ride, 5, 11. *See also* Neuro-rider training

Transverse abdominal muscles, 37

Tumors, 39

U

Uhl, Christian, 41

Utricle (utriculus), *33, 34*, 130

V

Vagus nerve, 83, 125

Valsalva maneuver, 37

Varifocal lens, 104

Vertigo, 23–24

Vestibular dysfunctions, 21, 33

Vestibular nuclei, 34, 72

Vestibular system, 33–34, *33*, 126–137. *See also* Balance and equilibrium training

Vestibulo-Ocular Reflex in Eight Directions, 132–134, *134*

Vibration on the Teeth, 70, *70*

Vision drills, 102–125

    Air Hunger Drills, 121

    for anxiety, 125

    background, 30–32, 103–104

    Binasal/Uninasal Partial Occlusion, 123–124, *124*

    concussions and, 114, 121

    Cross-o-Matic, 114–115, *114*, *116*, 125

    earplugs and, 124–125, *125*

    effective dose, 104, 115

    Eye Circles, 117–118, *117*

    Gaze Stabilization in Nine Points, *106*, 107–108

    Gentle Gaze Tracking in Eight Directions, 108–110, *108–109*, 125

    glasses (colored), 123, *123*, 124–125

    glasses (pinhole), 122–123, *122*, 124–125

    glasses (prescription), 103–104

    inhibition, instead of inactivation, 121

    Near-Far Jumps, 120, *120–121*, 125, 145

    Peripheral Vision training, 118–119, *118–119*

    Reflexive Eye Movements, 112, *112–113*

    Saccades, 110–111, *110*, 112–113, 145

    vision defined, 30, 32

    worksheet, 105

Visual dysfunctions, 18–19

Visualization and, 40

Visual system, 30–32, 34

Voluntary breathing, 37–38

W

Walk the Line, 49, 59, *59*

Y

Yes-Yes Movement (Flexion and Extension of the Cervical Spine), 78, *78*

Z

Zombie Stand, 49, 55, 56–57, *56*

Zombie Stand variations, 57–59, *57–58*

Z-Vibe tool, 70